POINT PARK

Private Smith's Journal

GENERAL WILLIAM T. SHERMAN

The Lakeside Classics

PRIVATE SMITH'S
JOURNAL

Recollections of the Late War

EDITED BY
CLYDE C. WALTON

The Lakeside Press

R. R. DONNELLEY & SONS COMPANY

CHICAGO

Christmas, 1963

PUBLISHERS' PREFACE

DURING the centennial commemoration of the
American Civil War it has been the Publishers' purpose to select for The Lakeside Classics
eye-witness accounts of that great historical drama
portraying several theaters of operation seen from
differing points of view. So far, we have included
books dealing with the Army of the Potomac, the
Army of Northern Virginia, and the little known
New Mexico campaign of 1861 and 1862 in the West.
This year we turn to a hitherto unpublished manuscript that describes the fighting in the central West,
including the battles around Atlanta; quite likely
the decisive theater of the war.

We have chosen the diary of a young resident of
Kankakee, Illinois, who enlisted early in the war
and served out two enlistments in the Union Army
of the Cumberland. He was involved in most of the
great battles of this area, except for Shiloh, Stones
River, and Grant's campaigns around Vicksburg.
He was present at Corinth, Murfreesboro, Chickamauga; marched to Knoxville, participated in the
battles of Sherman's campaign to Atlanta, and returned finally to Nashville with Thomas' army in
pursuit of Hood. To bring each part of Smith's
personal narrative into perspective with the overall
campaign, we requested the Editor, Mr. Clyde C.
Walton, to precede each chapter with a brief intro-

duction that outlines for the reader the significance of the action described.

The Company is pleased to report another successful year for the business. Our new plants mentioned in previous volumes have matured, and are making satisfactory contributions to the business. Our expansion program is on schedule. The installation of four large new presses in Chicago, designed for the production of *The New Yorker* magazine which begins in the spring of 1964, has been completed. Thus another material addition to our Chicago operation is added to the many others made since the war. Other large new presses have been placed in operation in several of our other plants this year, and more press capacity is being installed for initial operation in 1964.

We wish to express our gratitude once again to our customers old and new, and to our suppliers and many other friends for their confidence in us, and for their fine cooperation in our mutual undertakings; and to our employees we express our warm thanks for the loyal and fine performance that has contributed so greatly toward winning and holding the favorable regard of those who have entrusted us with their printing requirements.

To all, a Merry Christmas and a Prosperous and Happy New Year!

THE PUBLISHERS

Christmas, 1963

CONTENTS

HISTORICAL INTRODUCTION

THE Civil War journal of Benjamin T. Smith is the record kept by an unsophisticated 18-year-old of his services in the Civil War, from October, 1861, to November, 1865. Smith's journal differs from most journals kept by privates because he saw the war from two different levels—as a simple soldier who endured the rough discomforts, the miserable food, the occasional moments of great danger, and the fleeting times of fellowship around the fire, and as a member of a division headquarters, carrying important messages, acting as a mounted scout, serving as General Phil Sheridan's orderly.

Benjamin T. Smith's journal is one of the more than 250,000 Civil War manuscripts in the Illinois State Historical Library. The journal was presented to the Library by Mr. Joseph R. Wood, who is a great-nephew of Smith's; and we are deeply indebted to him for preserving this remarkably human document. Unfortunately, Private Smith is like so many other Americans who left civilian life, joined the Union Army—in every case serving to the best of their ability, and then returned to the anonymity of civilian life. This is to say, not much is known about Benjamin T. Smith.

We do know that he was born on February 27, 1844, in Providence, Rhode Island, to Benjamin K. and Sarah Smith. His father was a shoemaker by trade, and the family lived in Providence until perhaps 1856, then moved to Haverhill, Massachusetts, and later to Kankakee, Illinois. Whether his father died or was separated from his wife before the family came to Illinois we do not know; Benjamin does not ever mention his father in his journal. There were six children in the family; and at the time Benjamin enlisted, Mary S. was twenty-five; Joseph F., twenty-one; Calvin R., fifteen; Julia E., twelve; Walter E., seven. Their mother was forty-three.

When he enrolled for service on September 20, 1861, Smith described himself as being a resident of Kankakee, Illinois; a student and painter by occupation; 5 feet 6½ inches in height, with blue eyes, dark hair, and a fair complexion (in 1903 he described himself as being an inch taller, weighing 160 pounds, with dark hazel eyes, gray hair, a florid complexion, and a scar over his left eye). He enlisted in the small town of Watseka. The 51st Regiment, of which his company became a part, was accepted into federal service December 24, 1861, at Camp Douglas, Chicago. But for about eight months in 1862–1863 Smith was in an irregular mounted infantry unit and he mentions being elected 8th corporal and later 3rd corporal—as far as all official records are concerned, he enlisted as a private, served the whole war as a private, and was discharged a private. There are no surviving records, however, for "Powell's Scouts," the irregular unit with which he served—so why doubt his promotions?

The regimental records in the Illinois State Archives are also silent concerning Smith's later service, showing him only as detached to division headquarters. But he was mustered out, with Company C of the 51st, at Camp Butler in Springfield, Illinois, on September 25, 1865.

Apparently he lived in Chicago in 1866, then went to Providence, Rhode Island, for a time, returning to Chicago in 1867; in 1868 he lived at 572 Fulton Street and was a partner in the firm of Barger & Smith, "trunks, valises and traveling bags, 124 E. Randolph." In 1869 the company expanded to include manufacturing as well as sales, operating from 85 Clark Street as well as the Randolph Street address. In 1870 Smith had his own company, B. T. Smith and Company, in conjunction with a C. S. Brown; they were located at the old Randolph Street address and at 137 West Adams, and seem to have been trunk manufacturers only. In 1872 the directories show him still in the same business, but without a firm name, and with a new address on State Street; in 1873 he was located on Madison Street. In 1874, his last year in Chicago, he apparently had left the trunk manufacturing business and was working for the Chicago Omnibus Company. Some time in 1874 or early in 1875 he moved to St. Louis, where he spent the rest of his life.

On May 2, 1868, he was married in St. Mary's Church, Chicago, to Miss Mary Elizabeth Doyle; his journal at no point indicates any formal church affil-

iation, although it does demonstrate his belief in
God; in view of what evidence exists, we must assume that he was, or in 1868 became, a Catholic. His
wife was some four years younger than he, and their
union was blessed by three children: Francis Albert,
born in 1878; Will Leon, born in 1881; a daughter
Lulu, whose date of birth is not known and who pre-
ceded Smith in death.

In St. Louis, Smith was once again involved in
both the manufacture and sale of trunks; the St.
Louis directory of 1876 lists him as foreman for the
B. A. Hickman Company (they were trunk manufacturers), and in 1886 he was listed as a salesman
for the P. C. Murphy Trunk Company. In 1908 he
was in the directory as a traveling salesman. He
died on January 20 of that year and was buried
from St. Teresa's Church in Calvary Cemetery,
being survived by his wife Mary. He seems to have
been a man of unremarkable attainments, but,
withal, a man who lived a simple, useful life. Perhaps the high point in his life (we will never really
know) was his diligent but unspectacular Civil War
army career.

Smith's army service took him from rural Watseka to Chicago and then to the great depot and
staging area of Cairo, Illinois; to New Madrid and
Island No. 10 in Missouri; to Shiloh; to Corinth,
Mississippi; to northern Alabama, Georgia, and
Tennessee. In Tennessee, Smith was quartered
in Nashville and scouted its surrounding territory;

he knew Murfreesboro, Chickamauga, and Chatta-
nooga; and he would march to Knoxville in east
Tennessee. Next he moved south with Sherman to
Atlanta, via Tunnel Hill, Buzzard's Roost, Rocky
Face Ridge, Resaca, New Hope Church, Acworth,
Kenesaw Mountain, Peach Tree Creek, and Love-
joy's Station. Finally, back to Nashville after Hood:
Lynnville, Columbia, Spring Hill, Franklin, and
Nashville.

Most of Smith's two enlistments were served out
in the Army of the Cumberland; he arrived too late
to fight at Shiloh, although he did inch along with
Halleck's command in the investiture of Corinth.
Except for the Battle of Stone's River (and Grant's
campaigns around Vicksburg) he was involved in all
the great battles in the West: Chickamauga, Chattanooga, the advance to Atlanta, and return to Tennessee after Hood's army.

Benjamin T. Smith's war was like no war that had
been fought before and was like no war that would
be fought in the future. But then no war is ever like
any other war except that all are created by men and
fought and won, or fought and lost, by men. The
men are the same. The form of war changes: the uniforms, the drills, the food (never more than ade-
quate, and often less), the weapons, the modes of
transportation, all of the physical accoutrements of
war change. But in the end, the single most important factor is the character of the men involved, particularly the character of the men who lead. War is

the great test of the character of man; the Civil War —Smith's war—is no exception.

One of the greatest mistakes we can make today in studying the Civil War is to attempt to understand it in terms of our contemporary society and our contemporary military knowledge. It is hardly possible to compare our organized twentieth-century society with its instantaneous communications; its national organizations for business, commerce, education, politics, philanthropy, entertainment; and its indisputably formalized national government with the unorganized, slower-moving society of a century ago, less formal in structure, but more formal in social intercourse; with a federal government clearly disputable as to basic authority and function; and with almost no concept of national organization in other areas of human endeavor.

Less comparable yet is the Army of the Cumberland with any of its modern counterparts. The difference clearly reflects our increased organization at every level of the army. The soldier in our modern infantry division has more formal education and a greater knowledge (but not awareness) of his country and the world; he is enlisted (or perhaps drafted) by the national, not the state, government; the raising and recruiting of armies is now unquestionably a federal prerogative. Our diarist Benjamin T. Smith, however, was enlisted in his home community by the state of Illinois; his unit was later accepted for federal service by the federal government and only then became a part of the Union Army. In the Civil War, recruiting was handled by the states at the request of the federal government: the federal government assigned quotas, and it was the responsibility of the state to find the required number of men.

Smith's officers at the company level were originally elected by the members of their company (this practice was generally followed at the beginning of the war but was often abandoned as the war progressed); our modern officers are the product of substantial and prolonged military training. Smith's equipment was rudimentary, frequently of poor quality; his housing was equally poor; his rifle was a foreign import, heavy, awkward, and unreliable; his food was issued directly to him and he was his own cook (as a consequence, small groups of men—very descriptively called a "mess"—cooked together). The food he received was highly salted, most often fried or roasted—from the standpoint of nutrition completely out of balance. Much of the time in enemy territory he took what food he could find—from farm, field, or larder. In contrast, our soldier today has a rifle identical with that used by all other U.S. soldiers; he has well-designed and well-manufactured clothing; he uses central mess facilities, serving wholesome, balanced meals, and in the field equally balanced rations are issued to him.

The basic military unit in the Civil War was the infantry regiment. The word regiment suggests a splendid and exciting martial picture: a mass of men in bright uniforms, arrayed in long straight lines, with flags bravely flying, their faces to the enemy. Smith's regiment was the 51st Illinois Infantry, and he was in Company C; the regiment had several nicknames—the "Ryan Life Guard" and the "Chicago Legion" (although only one of the companies was from Cook County). C company was from Iroquois County, and the men in the other companies were drawn from twelve additional Illinois counties. Like all Union infantry regiments, the 51st Illinois when at maximum strength had 1,025 officers and men. The ten companies of 101 men each were numbered A, B, C, D, E, F, G, H, I, and K. Actually Smith's regiment was formed from a number of independent small companies which the governor of Illinois ordered combined to form the 51st. For example, the "Union Railroad Guard" became Company A, the "Tucker Light Guard" became Company B, Smith's Iroquois County unit became Company C, the "Fremont Fencibles" became Company K, and the "Sturgis Light Guard" became Company E. At full strength, each company had one captain, one first lieutenant, one second lieutenant, one first sergeant, four sergeants, eight corporals, two musicians, a wagoner, and eighty-two privates. The regiment was commanded by a colonel; the staff upon which he could call for advice and assistance in handling his men consisted of two musicians, a hospital steward, a commissary sergeant, a quartermaster sergeant, a sergeant major, a chaplain, two assistant surgeons, a surgeon who ranked as a major, a quartermaster, an adjutant, a major, and a lieutenant colonel. In practice, privates from the companies were assigned to regimental headquarters for orderly, scout, messenger, and housekeeping duties; higher headquarters also drew their personnel from the infantry regiments. As a matter of fact, it was unusual to find a regiment on active duty with anything like 1,025 men. Indeed, a unit would be accepted into U.S. service with as few as 845 officers and men (in such cases the number of privates was reduced from 82 to 64 per company). Smith's Company C had 93 officers and men when mustered into federal service: of these 93, 74 were privates. For comparison, on June 1, 1945, an infantry company totaled 235 enlisted men, and a full regiment had more than 3,500 enlisted men.

Just as it took ten companies to make a regiment, it took two or more regiments to make a brigade (in 1862, General Sheridan commanded a brigade in Missouri, composed of a regiment from Michigan and a regiment from Iowa, with a total strength of 827 men; a few months later he commanded another brigade composed of four regiments, the 2nd and 15th Missouri and the 36th and 44th Illinois). The next higher unit was the division, which was composed of a number of brigades; Sheridan's first divisional command was the 11th. It had three brigades, each with four regiments, plus two attached batteries of artillery: the 35th Brigade (the 44th and

73rd Illinois and the 2nd and 15th Missouri), the 36th Brigade (the 85th, 86th, and 125th Illinois and the 52nd Ohio), the 37th Brigade (the 36th and 88th Illinois, the 21st Michigan, and the 24th Wisconsin), the 2nd Illinois Light Battery I, and the 1st Missouri Light Battery G. One more step up the hierarchy is to corps (two or more divisions) and then to army (two or more corps). In practice, however, the Union Army was informal in organization as well as in discipline.

At different periods of the war, a man could enlist for 3 months, for 6 months, for 9 months, for 1 year, 2 years, or 3 years. There was no social stigma attached to serving out one's enlistment and then going home to resume civilian life even though the war was still being fought. If a regiment (or a high percentage of its members) re-enlisted *en masse,* its men were entitled to call themselves veteran volunteers. Thus, in January and February of 1864, when the 51st Illinois generally re-enlisted, Smith and his friends became veteran volunteers. In fact, the Army of the Cumberland was handicapped at that time and again in June of 1864 because its officers had to spend so much time in urging regiments to re-enlist; if they were successful, the men had to be given re-enlistment furloughs and those who did not re-enlist had to be provided with transportation home. This ill-conceived system of enlistments, the later conscription with its discriminatory arrangement for the use of paid substitutes, and the raising of new regiments rather than filling the gaps caused by disease and battle casualties in old regiments, are all incomprehensible today. Together they constitute a strong indictment for inadequate planning and for mismanagement against both the Congress and Lincoln's administration.

If it is a mistake to study the Civil War in terms of our contemporary organized civilization, it is also a mistake to study Civil War army operations from maps alone. When we look at war on a map, everything is neat and orderly. The little rectangles mark the locations of regiments, brigades, corps, and armies; arrows show where the units moved and marched; at places where an arrow runs into a rectangle, fighting took place; the arrows trace the battle movements and finally show which units retired and the direction they followed. Perhaps this rather tidy paper war is useful in helping us understand the larger movements of great armies, but the maps somehow emasculate war and so never reveal the whole story.

Wars are not fought on a flat, card-table surface but on the ground; and whatever the configuration of terrain, it is never dead level or absolutely clear of obstructions. Battles, in fact, seem to have an affinity for places that abound in swamps, fast rivers, rough hills, narrow passes, dense woods; with weather that is stifling hot or mercilessly cold, where it rains too often or where sleet and snow coat the ground, where insect pests make an already miserable existence almost unendurable. The map cannot show the wretchedness of the private soldier, dirty, soaked to the skin, shivering over a smoky fire deep in the woods, trying to keep dry, warm; a piece of salt pork on the end of his ramrod held over the flame and a biscuit of hardtack out of the rain under his shirt. This soldier and hundreds of others, equally miserable, appear on the map only as a neat geometrical figure. The map, however, does demonstrate what did happen at a particular place.

It is worth remembering that the officers on both sides in the Civil War employed the same tactics, for many of them were trained at the same school—West Point—and many of them had fought together in the war with Mexico. It is not surprising, therefore, that they had the same idea about how best to defeat an opposing army. The basic maneuvers were quite simple: both sides formed battle lines when a major engagement seemed near. The lines were not straight because of the nature of the terrain; either they bent around in front of or over the crest of a hill; they bent around behind a swamp; they bent around a cleared field in a forest; they bent forward, perhaps, to include a road junction or crossroads. The lines were never absolutely continuous. That is, the last soldier on the far right (or right flank) of Regiment X might or might not be within sight or sound of the left flank of Regiment Y, the next regiment in line. In front of the main line were outposts and pickets whose principal function was to guard against surprise attack; behind the line was the reserve, to be used to bolster a weak part of the line or to push back a momentarily successful attack that had broken through the line; because of its mobility its presence was a constant threat to the enemy. Also behind the line were all the house-keeping and supply services—the engineers, the medics, the long wagon trains, various headquarters, the mobile telegraph equipment, the supply dumps.

Supplies (which mean everything the soldier needed to keep alive and fighting) were brought by railroad to the rear of the army. Ammunition, food, clothing, spare parts, or what have you, were loaded on wagons and taken right to the army from the nearest point on the railroad. If no railroad was near, supplies were brought by steamboat and then by wagon. In bad weather and through the winter the condition of the roads was all important; they had to be kept open if the army was not to starve and go naked. Reinforcements came over the same route, as did the telegraph lines and all communications. Thousands of men were involved in keeping the supply routes open. These included men from the quartermaster corps as well as many others from the fighting regiments who acted not only as guards but as porters and construction crews.

It is obvious why military men have always been preoccupied with the idea of getting to the rear of the opposing army. If a really large force can be put behind the enemy, he is immediately deprived of all

food and ammunition supplies, he loses all communications with his superiors, and he has to face an
enemy coming from a direction other than that his
fortifications were built to command. Since the enemy is well aware of how bad things will be if you get
behind him (and he probably has been scheming to
get behind you), he particularly guards against such
a threat. Rarely did large infantry forces get in the
enemy rear during the Civil War. Instead, fast-moving cavalry forces raided around the extreme ends
(flanks) of the line, harassing and burning wagon
trains, destroying bridges, indulging in the great
Civil War sport of tearing up the railroad tracks.

These raiding cavalry forces were organized into
regiments and corps and generally—although not
always—assigned to an army commander. The Union cavalry regiment was a little larger than an infantry regiment; usually it had twelve companies of
100 men each, but like the infantry regiment it was
almost never at full strength. The Union cavalry
was generally inferior to Confederate cavalry until
late in 1864, when several remarkable cavalry units
were organized—led by Generals Phil Sheridan,
James Harrison Wilson, and Alfred Pleasonton.
Throughout Smith's tour of duty the Army of the
Cumberland had to cope with Confederate cavalry
led by the superior Nathan B. Forrest, the romantic
John Hunt Morgan, and the hard-hitting Joe Wheeler. In addition to serving as a highly mobile striking
force, cavalry troops were used for scouting, for

screening troop movements, and for courier duty. Large-scale engagements of cavalry against cavalry were rare; the largest was in the Gettysburg campaign at Brandy Station, June 9, 1863; the other important clash was at Yellow Tavern, May 11, 1864, near Richmond, Virginia. Large cavalry units almost never lined up and charged in one long line with sabers drawn; most cavalrymen never used a saber for any purpose more dangerous than chopping kindling or opening an ammunition box; indeed, many cavalrymen were never issued sabers. In action, cavalry moved quickly to their objective, where they dismounted and fought on foot, using their short-barreled carbines.

The other important fighting unit was the artillery. The light artillery regiment, when at full strength, consisted of twelve batteries (companies) of 150 men and six guns, but usually a battery had four guns. The batteries almost always operated as independent commands—which is to say, the artillery regiment never fought as a regiment. Rather, its batteries were attached to regiments or higher commands. There were many kinds and makes of artillery weapons and many types of ammunition; range was limited and (except for mortars) artillery fired directly at a target that the gunners could see. In fact, artillery was often right up with the infantry rifle companies and sometimes in front of them. Duels between individual guns or batteries were common, and since light artillery could be moved with good speed in fair weather, units often accompanied cavalry columns on raids. Today the artilleryman rarely sees what he is shooting at; using mathematical calculations, he fires on a crossroads miles away or at enemy emplacements far out of his sight; the Civil War artilleryman actually saw his target, sighted his gun, and let fly.

The artillery could be horribly effective when using grape or canister at close range (in effect turning the cannon into a huge shotgun); or, when using solid shot or shells, for destroying or forcing an enemy battery out of action (counter battery fire), firing upon and destroying (reducing) fortifications, or shelling infantry or cavalry in the open. With the artillery in the open, right up on the line with the infantry, and exposed to heavy enemy rifle fire, casualties were generally higher than those expected today.

All through the Civil War, surprise was a tactic both sides tried to use, but like many military maneuvers, it was easy to plan on a map under the yellow lantern light in the general's tent, but difficult to achieve in practice. Rarely was planned surprise using large forces achieved in a major battle, but with the rigidity of purpose demonstrated by the oriental mystic who spends years in contemplation of his navel, generals on both sides kept hoping, and their determination produced results occasionally enough to keep everyone trying. But the successes usually came only in scouting, patrolling, raiding, and other small actions. One reason surprise attacks were difficult to effect in major battles was that it was almost impossible to keep major troop movements secret. Before a planned attack, sufficient forces were concentrated so as to outnumber the enemy greatly at the point where the attack would begin. In dry weather concentrating troops raised great clouds of dust which hung over the moving columns like arrows pointing from the sky. In bad weather everything—men, animals, wagons—bogged down, and the whole maneuver took so long that it was certain to be discovered. And in any weather there were always spies, scouts, deserters, and cavalry patrols, all hazards to large-scale troop maneuvers.

There are many ways to make an attack, and many were used in the Civil War. If the enemy army was concentrated into one long line, the whole line could be assaulted at once and the reserve rushed through any weak spot that might be found, being turned to the right or left (or both) and attacking the rest of the line from the rear and side. The enemy reserve, of course, was rushed to the point where the breakthrough occurred, but the attack might continue if they were slow in arriving or insufficient in numbers. A second standard attack plan was to concentrate heavily at one end of the line—let us, for the sake of example, say the right—and have either a weak or fake attack take place on the left, hoping to lure the enemy reserves to that end. The major attack was then ordered in on the right and if it broke the defense line, it would turn to the left and attack down and behind the length of the enemy line. At this time a general assault would be ordered all along the front. In outline, this is the attack planned by General Thomas at the Battle of Nashville in which Private Smith participated. Many times during the Civil War one side outnumbered the other but for a variety of reasons was not able to make use of its numerical superiority in launching a successful attack: orders did not reach the proper officer, or were slow in arriving or were misunderstood; troops did not arrive on time or where expected; indecision or timidity made the commander hold back an unreasonably large number of reserves. Not bringing all available fighting forces to bear at the time of attack was responsible during the war for more "lost victories" than any other tactical flaw.

A third favored tactic was to defeat the enemy in detail. To explain, let us suppose that the outnumbered enemy, which we will call "A," is retreating, or appearing to retreat, through the mountains; the pursuing army, which we will call "B," splits its forces and gives chase through three different passes. But A has concentrated its forces in a valley behind the first ranges of hills and plans to attack the pursuing columns of B one at a time, where A's concentrated force outnumbers any single one of B's three columns. If A can overwhelm B's center column, he can then turn and attack either the left or right column of B's army and defeat it, too. At the very least, by defeating one of B's columns, he has cut down B's advantage of numerical superiority. General Bragg planned this kind of attack on Rosecrans' Union army for what turned into the Battle of Chickamauga.

A fourth plan of attack was often used when the principal objective was a terrain feature or city rather than the enemy army. With this strategy it is possible to capture the objective without fighting a major battle. Assume that the enemy (A) is defending a city by trying to bring on a battle under his terms at a site far from the city. If the attacking army (B) has numerical superiority, B moves forward until the enemy (A) is located, well entrenched in a chain of low hills. B can then follow one of two lines of action. He can march his army far around one flank or the other, and if successful force A to leave his prepared positions and withdraw to avoid having his communications cut (the attacking army of B must be careful on the march not to present any opportunity for A to attack him). The other line of action is for B to approach the entrenched positions of A and demonstrate against them. Using his superior numbers, B then begins to extend, let us say for the sake of example, his left flank, continuing to add units to the left, stretching his line farther and farther until it goes beyond A's prepared defenses. If A extends his flank to parallel that of the attacking army, he is spreading himself so thin that weak spots will develop quickly. Rather than continuing to match B's extension to the left (a game which A cannot win), A must either attack or withdraw. Since his opponent B has more men, as well as a solid line without weak spots, and can quickly draw in his extended flank if an attack develops, the defender A has little choice but to withdraw. As A withdraws to another good defensive position, however, he hopes his attacker B will pursue rashly and offer his army the opportunity to turn and attack. General Sherman as the attacker used both these tactics in his summer of 1864 campaign towards Atlanta, maneuvering General Johnston out of his prepared positions and forcing him to continue to fall back towards the city.

Obviously many factors enter into either a successful attack or defense. At the Battle of Chickamauga, for example, the railroad was used to bring General Longstreet's men from the eastern theatre to Georgia, so that the Confederates suddenly had more men in their army than the Union commander had. The nature of enemy entrenchments also affects the outcome of battles. At the beginning of the war a few military men believed that entrenching was somehow not sporting, perhaps even cowardly, but this nonsense disappeared in the stern test of battle. Unbelievably high casualties resulted from attacks made frontally on well-dug–in troops who had plenty of ammunition and artillery support. So, for example, Sherman found out when he attacked the Confederate Kenesaw Mountain positions in his Atlanta campaign—the one time before

the city was reached that he substituted frontal
attack for maneuver.

The operations in which our diarist Benjamin T.
Smith found himself engaged are hard to understand unless we know what the other Union and
Confederate armies were doing at the same time.
Why did Smith have to leave his pleasant job of
guarding the railroad in northern Alabama and go
north? Because a Confederate army was invading
Kentucky. Why leave hard-won Chattanooga and go
to Knoxville in east Tennessee? Because a strong Confederate force led by General Longstreet was attacking General Burnside's Union army in that place.
So that the reader may better understand where
Smith was and why his army did what it did, some
review of operations in the West may prove helpful.

It is important to remember that there was no
"Berlin wall" across the United States during the
Civil War, no fortified line from east to west across
the nation behind which the opposing armies could
crouch, ready to spring out and attack when an opportunity offered a chance of success. Rather, the
Civil War was a war in which a number of armies op-
posed each other; if the Confederates had an army in
Kentucky, the Union quickly put an army in Kentucky to oppose them; if the Confederates threatened
east Tennessee, the Union put together an army and
hurried it to that area. But there were large areas of
the country not occupied in force by either side, or
at most by small troop units or fast-moving cavalry

patrols. Where armies confronted each other directly, there were trenches, fortifications, artillery emplacements, and the other standard trappings of conventional war, but elsewhere there were thousands of small nameless clashes; neither side could be absolutely certain who controlled what part of this open territory at any specific moment.

The part of the war covered by Smith's journal is the West, and to avoid total confusion the reader must bear in mind (1) the geography of Kentucky, Tennessee, northern Alabama, and Georgia, because the different armies fought over this ground several times; (2) the frequent changes of high command and the shuffling and regrouping of armies on both sides; and (3) the relationship of these armies to each other as well as to other campaigns being fought in the other theatres of war.

The war in the West began in September of 1861 when the Confederate command, ill advised, breached Kentucky neutrality by fortifying Columbus, Kentucky, some eighteen miles down the Mississippi River from Cairo, Illinois. At that time the Confederate command structure was this: General Albert Sidney Johnston was in charge of Confederate forces in the area covered by this journal, with his right at Knoxville, Tennessee, and Cumberland Gap—under Brigadier General Felix K. Zollicoffer; his center at Bowling Green, Kentucky—under Major General William J. Hardee and Brigadier General Simon Bolivar Buckner; and his left anchored on the Tennessee, Cumberland, and Mississippi rivers. Major General Leonidas Polk was at Columbus, Kentucky, and additional troops were at Fort Henry on the Tennessee River and Fort Donelson on the Cumberland River; and at New Madrid, Missouri, Island No. 10, and Fort Pillow (in Tennessee), all on the Mississippi River.

On the Union side the overall command was vested in General Winfield Scott in Washington, who was succeeded November 1, 1861, by Major General George B. McClellan. In the West, the first commander had been Major General John C. Fremont, who was succeeded by Major General David Hunter, and then, on November 19, 1861, by General Henry W. Halleck. Brigadier General Grant was commanding at Cairo, Illinois; Brigadier General William T. Sherman's Army of the Ohio was lined up against Hardee's troops at Bowling Green; Brigadier General George H. Thomas was watching Zollicoffer in east Tennessee. After the useless Battle of Belmont (November 7, 1861) fought by Grant in Missouri (across the Mississippi River from Columbus, Kentucky) and after the more important battle between Crittenden and Thomas at Mill Springs, Kentucky (January 19, 1862), which resulted in a Confederate retreat out of east Tennessee and Zollicoffer's death, several command changes took place. Brigadier General Don Carlos Buell replaced Sherman, and Confederate General P. G. T. Beauregard came from the East to be second in command to Johnston.

The first significant Union military advance in the West took place in February, 1862; Grant moved to attack Fort Henry on the Tennessee River. The fort surrendered on February 6 to Commodore Andrew H. Foote's gunboats before Grant's infantry could make an assault, but Grant moved on to Fort Donelson on the Cumberland River. After a nasty, hard fight, the fort capitulated, on February 16, 1862, to his "unconditional surrender" ultimatum. These two actions began a career for Grant that would take him to the White House. (No one paid much attention then, but at the Fort Donelson surrender an obscure Confederate cavalry colonel led his men out of the fort in time to evade capture. His name was Nathan Bedford Forrest, and he would be a constant thorn in the side to Union commanders for the rest of the war. There is no question that he is the best cavalry leader ever produced on the North American continent.)

With the fall of Fort Henry, the Tennessee River was opened to Northern gunboats all the way to Nashville, and so Hardee retired slowly from Bowling Green, Kentucky, through Nashville to Murfreesboro, Tennessee, followed all the way by General Buell, who occupied unfortified Nashville on February 24–25.

The next successful Union attack was launched against the Confederate position on the Mississippi River at New Madrid, Missouri, and Island No. 10, which Halleck ordered Brigadier General John Pope to take. Private Smith's 51st Illinois was a part of

Pope's force—in Colonel Gilbert W. Cumming's 2nd Brigade of Brigadier General E. A. Paine's 4th Division. The Union troops saw little action, however, since New Madrid was evacuated on the 14th of March and Island No. 10—being upstream of New Madrid (even though it was south of the city) and caught between federal gunboats above and Union artillery at New Madrid below—capitulated on April 7. Smith's regiment pursued the Confederates along their only escape route, the road to Tiptonville, Tennessee.

General Johnston, meanwhile, had concentrated his troops at Corinth, Mississippi, abandoning Columbus, Kentucky, and being reinforced by troops under Major General Braxton Bragg. At the same time, Grant was moving up the Tennessee River to Pittsburg Landing. Now, with Buell's army marching west across Tennessee to join Grant, Johnston attacked Grant at Pittsburg Landing; the battle took its name from a small church near the landing: Shiloh. The argument still rages as to why Grant had not fortified his positions and as to the degree he had been caught off guard. On April 6, 1862, the first day of battle, the Union troops were almost driven into the river, but they rallied, and at dusk were still holding on. Buell's army crossed the river during the night, and the combined Union forces attacked the next day (April 7), finally forcing the Confederates (now commanded by Beauregard because Johnston had been killed on the first day) from the field.

The Battle of Shiloh was the largest engagement fought on the continent up to that time; the Confederates lost something over 10,000 men killed, wounded, and missing, the Union about 13,000.

The Southern troops withdrew behind the defenses of Corinth, where they were joined by troops under Generals Earl Van Dorn and Sterling Price. At this point in the campaign there were about 50,-000 Confederate soldiers at Corinth. The Union forces were now directly commanded by Halleck, with Grant as second in command; Thomas led the right, and his troops were designated the Army of the Tennessee; Buell led the center, designated the Army of the Ohio; and Pope the left, designated the Army of the Mississippi. The Union troops totaled perhaps 125,000.

Smith and the 51st Illinois arrived at Pittsburg Landing on April 21 and took part in the advance towards Corinth; during this march they were at Farmington, Mississippi, on the two occasions when Beauregard lashed out at Pope's advanced position there. Beauregard had little real hope, however, of holding back the Union might; and when Halleck's tediously slow, over-cautious advance threatened to become an all-out attack against Corinth, the Confederates, on May 29, skillfully began to retire to Tupelo, Mississippi, some fifty miles away. Two new cavalry leaders emerged from the Shiloh-Corinth campaign: Confederate Colonel John Hunt Morgan was promoted brigadier general in December and

Union Colonel Phil Sheridan became a brigade commander, and would soon be promoted brigadier general.

After the Shiloh-Corinth campaign General Bragg replaced Beauregard, and decided to move to the north and "invade" Kentucky, using not only the army at Tupelo but Major General Edmund Kirby Smith's troops in east Tennessee. The great Union Army at Corinth was separated into several independent commands: Grant and Buell stayed in the west throughout the summer, but Major General Pope was sent east to lead the Army of Virginia, and Halleck went east in July to take overall command of Union forces. Early in the summer Buell was ordered to march from Corinth, Mississippi, to east Tennessee and to repair the vital Memphis and Charleston Railroad on the route. Smith and the 51st Illinois were with Buell, and from July 26 to September 27 their duty consisted of guarding the rebuilt railroad in the Trinity Station–Decatur, Alabama, area; Buell's main force was then halted at Stevenson, Alabama. When Bragg launched his Kentucky campaign, he ordered General Hardee to take the army from Tupelo to Chattanooga; Major General Sterling Price would stay in Mississippi to oppose Grant's army. (Confederate cavalry was particularly effective in the last six months of 1862; led by Generals Morgan, Forrest, and Joseph Wheeler, the fast-moving cavalrymen raided all through Tennessee and Kentucky.)

As Bragg's plan unfolded, General Smith moved north from Knoxville and on August 30, 1862, won the hard-fought battle of Richmond, Kentucky, practically destroying Major General William Nelson's command. Smith then occupied Frankfort and Lexington, Kentucky, and threatened Louisville and Cincinnati, Ohio. On August 28 Bragg started north from Chattanooga with an army of two wings, one led by Hardee (with Major General Simon Bolivar Buckner as second in command), the other by Polk. Buell made his countermoves carefully, first to Murfreesboro, Tennessee, and then to Nashville, which was already strongly fortified. There he left only a division under Brigadier General James S. Negley and then followed Bragg north into Kentucky.

Smith and the 51st, ordered to rejoin Buell, left Decatur, Alabama, on September 27. During the march to Nashville, Smith was somehow absorbed into an impromptu, irregular unit of mounted infantrymen called "Powell's Scouts," and he served with them for the next eight months, scouting, patrolling, and doing escort duty around Nashville. There "Powell's Scouts" often ran into Confederate pickets and cavalry detachments, sometimes precipitating small but nonetheless deadly actions at such places as Stewart's Ferry at Stone's River.

Smith, then, was not further involved in the campaign in Kentucky, but a word about this campaign is necessary because it provides the background for all of the actions he would be in during the rest of the war.

Bragg wasted his time in Kentucky, issuing proclamations and installing a Confederate governor at Frankfort but never concentrating his forces for an effective military move. Buell meanwhile was getting reinforcements from Grant's army in Mississippi (by river, through Louisville), including Brigadier General Sheridan, whose star was rising; he would command a division from now on.

Neither Grant nor Sherman, however, figured in the Tennessee campaigns until after the fall of Vicksburg in July, 1863. In June, 1862, when Fort Pillow was evacuated by the Confederates and Memphis was occupied by Union troops, Vicksburg remained the only Confederate barrier along the entire length of the Mississippi River; Vicksburg would therefore be their target. During the difficult fighting in Tennessee, Grant and Sherman were trying to crack the hard nut of Vicksburg. But prior to the Vicksburg campaign two important actions were fought in Mississippi, at Iuka and Corinth. Thereafter Lieutenant General John C. Pemberton was assigned to the command at Vicksburg, with Van Dorn in charge of his cavalry; in December Van Dorn's raid against Grant's supply lines and depot at Holly Springs, Mississippi, helped stop the 1862 overland movement by Grant towards Vicksburg.

Back in Kentucky, Buell fought at Perryville on October 8 with a part of Bragg's army led by Polk, and the result was a Confederate victory. Bragg, curiously, did not attempt to exploit the victory (as he had likewise failed to do after another, earlier victory at Munfordville) and began a withdrawal toward Cumberland Gap to Knoxville in east Tennessee. General Smith's forces stayed at Knoxville, while the rest of Bragg's army concentrated at Murfreesboro, where it was joined by men under Generals Forrest and John C. Breckinridge; Buell had followed the retreat but was constantly frustrated by Wheeler's well-directed cavalry, and finally concentrated his army at Nashville. As so often happened after battle action, there were more command changes. Confederate General Smith ended up in charge of things west of the Mississippi River, and the extremely able General Joseph Eggleston Johnston was put in charge not only of the Tennessee troops but also of Pemberton's in and around Vicksburg. The Confederate President, Jefferson Davis, visited the army in Murfreesboro and Chattanooga in December and forced Johnston to send about 10,000 of his troops to Pemberton at Vicksburg. The major Confederate units left in Tennessee under Bragg at Murfreesboro were two corps under Polk and Hardee. The cavalry under Wheeler was responsible to Hardee, and it was units of Wheeler's cavalry that Smith ran into from time to time. On the Union side, Buell was replaced by Rosecrans, and the Army of the Cumberland was formed into three corps, commanded by Generals Thomas, Thomas L. Crittenden, and Alexander M. McCook. Rosecrans was given to understand that he was expected to attack as soon as he could.

And he did attack, beginning his movement towards Murfreesboro on December 26, arriving at Stone's River near the city on the 30th. Both sides decided to attack, and each decided to attack his opponent's right; the Confederates moved first, and, in the Battle of Murfreesboro (or Stone's River) on the 31st, were able to punish and push back several of Rosecrans' divisions, radically bending the Union line, but they could not follow up their initial success. No action of major significance took place on New Year's Day of 1863, and after inconclusive action on the 2nd of January, Bragg once again adopted his favorite tactic and began to retreat late on the 3rd. The Confederate cavalry continued to be active and Rosecrans did not pursue; Bragg got his troops back some twenty miles to Tullahoma (Hardee) and Shelbyville (Polk), and considerable discussion among his higher officers followed—a discussion concerning their total lack of confidence in their general's military ability. President Davis, however, would not remove him, and Bragg retained his command. Our journalist, Benjamin T. Smith, was not in this battle since "Powell's Scouts" were still patrolling the vicinity of Nashville.

From the Battle of Murfreesboro until the end of June all was quiet in Tennessee, except for cavalry actions. "Powell's Scouts" were disbanded, and Smith returned to Company C of the 51st Illinois. He stayed only a few days, however, and then was assigned as an orderly at Major General Philip Sheridan's division headquarters. By this time Sheridan had attracted favorable attention; his strong defense during the Confederate attack at Murfreesboro helped save the Union lines from disintegrating, and he was now marked for more responsibility. Not long before Rosecrans had begun to move toward Murfreesboro in December, Brigadier General John H. Morgan moved into Kentucky to interrupt Rosecrans' communications. This raid should not be confused with the dashing General's great Ohio raid of July, 1863, when his troops crossed the Ohio below Louisville and raced through southern Indiana and Ohio. The Ohio raid was spectacular and created considerable apprehension in the North, but was lacking in any appreciable military effect. Morgan and his men were finally captured and confined in the Ohio State Penitentiary at Columbus; although Morgan later escaped, he was never again to play a really important role in the war.

Rosecrans — after a long period of inactivity — marched out of Nashville on June 23, 1863, and very cleverly maneuvered so that Bragg had to retreat from his heavily fortified position at Tullahoma. What Rosecrans did was to fake an attack on Polk at Shelbyville, while the real advance was made around Hardee's right, to Manchester and Decherd. The maneuver went as planned, and Bragg had to draw back to Tullahoma. When the Union cut the railroad at Decherd, Bragg had to fall back again, to Decherd and Winchester; still again the Confederate Army went back, this time to Cowan and finally over the mountain to Chattanooga.

Rosecrans' army was now divided into three corps: the 20th, commanded by Major General Alexander M. McCook; the 14th, by Major General George H. Thomas; and the 21st, by Major General Thomas L. Crittenden. Sheridan's 3rd Division (with Smith at division headquarters) participated in the "Tullahoma" campaign as a part of the 20th Corps. A fourth unit, called the Reserve Corps, was commanded by Major General Gordon Granger.

The Confederates began to make command changes when their army reached safety at Chattanooga. Hardee was sent to Mississippi, and his place was taken by Lieutenant General Daniel H. Hill, transferred from the Army of Northern Virginia. Bragg was removed from Johnston's control and given responsibility for east Tennessee, until then under the control of Buckner. It had been decided by the Confederate high command in the East to send Lieutenant General James Longstreet (with two divisions, commanded by Generals John B. Hood and Lafayette McLaws, plus the artillery commanded by Brigadier General Edward Porter Alexander) by railroad to Tennessee. But the direct railroad connection was broken when Major General Ambrose E. Burnside advanced with the Army of the Ohio from Louisville and occupied Knoxville. Burnside had no trouble at Knoxville because General Buckner had been ordered to leave the city and fall back to a position north of Chattanooga. With the railroad broken at Knoxville, Longstreet's men would have to go through North Carolina to Atlanta and then north to Chattanooga to join Bragg, and consequently they were slow in arriving in Georgia.

The country over which the armies would fight is rough and mountainous, with the mountains running in parallel ridges from northeast to southwest. The creeks are fast and deep, and the Tennessee River is an even more impassable barrier. Chattanooga itself is dominated by this fast river at its north and west, and by the formidable mountains to the south; only to the northeast is there any reasonable approach to the town. It was this complex mountainous terrain with which both commanders would have to cope. To further confuse the picture, three states meet southwest of Chattanooga: Alabama, Georgia, and Tennessee.

What Rosecrans hoped to accomplish was to get around behind Bragg's army to the Resaca-Dalton area in Georgia, and cut the railroad to Atlanta. To do this he would have to get his army through the mountains, a hard job at best, but he seemed very sure of himself, partly because he believed the deliberately spread Confederate rumors that Bragg was in full retreat from Chattanooga to the south. Rosecrans therefore sent each of his three corps on a separate route through the mountains, the 21st on the left toward Chattanooga, the 14th in the center through the mountains toward Lafayette, Georgia, and the 20th on the right to the south and west toward Alpine, Georgia. Although Bragg had abandoned Chattanooga, he was not retreating but concentrating his army at Lafayette, behind Chickamauga Creek. From that point he hoped to throw the whole weight of his army against just one corps of the Army of the Cumberland. This was sound strategy, but somehow his attack did not come off as planned; the Union corps he selected to hit was Thomas's 14th, which was to be attacked when it came out of the mountains into a natural cul-de-sac called McLemore's Cove. But orders were not delivered on time, commanders were slow to move, mixups occurred, and Thomas saw the danger ahead in time to stop the advance of the 14th Corps and back it up into the mountains at Stevens Gap. Bragg then decided to attack Crittenden's 21st Corps, which was at Lee and Gordon's Mill on the Chickamauga, but there was confusion on the Confederate side as to just where Crittenden was, and after some fumbling around, the attack failed to materialize. On the 13th of September, Rosecrans suddenly realized that his army was in trouble, McCook's 20th Corps was 57 miles marching distance through the mountains from Thomas's 14th Corps. Consequently, he ordered a hurried concentration of the army at Thomas's position; Smith was with Sheridan's division at Alpine, having come through Bridgeport, Alabama, and Trenton, Georgia, and as the Union Army concentrated, he was marched to Chickamauga Valley through Stevens Gap. Bragg had brought Buckner's command into his army; Rosecrans had moved Granger's reserve to Rossville, south of Chattanooga.

Bragg's plan was to attack Crittenden on the Union left, but Rosecrans was worried about the left and kept extending it farther, so that the left was not quite where Bragg thought it would be. Thomas, too, had been extended somewhat to the left. In the afternoon of the 18th Major General John B. Hood arrived via railway with a number of Longstreet's eastern troops, and the battle was ready to begin. On the 19th fighting ranged up and down the line, with no particular advantage to either side. That night Longstreet arrived with more Confederate troops, and the plan was still to smash the Union left. The attack on the 20th would proceed with each division attacking in turn, beginning on the Union left; Rosecrans had strengthened his left, however, and drawn Granger in closer to the battlefield. When troops were shifted on the Union right during the battle, a gap developed, and Hood's men went right through the hole. Longstreet had them turn to the right and continue their attack. Those units of Rosecrans' army that tried to plug this hole—including Sheridan's division—were smashed aside, and soon all was confusion in the Union right and center. Smith was in the gap and was lucky enough to survive. As soon as he could, he retreated toward Chattanooga on the McFarland's

Gap Road, but he returned near the end of the day to the rear of Thomas's position at Horseshoe Ridge. In this position Thomas had repulsed every assault thrown at him by the Confederates (in addition to his own men, he had been reinforced by Granger and had also gathered together all the troops he could lay his hands on). Thomas's unyielding defense at Chickamauga saved Rosecrans' army from destruction and earned for him the sobriquet "Rock of Chickamauga." About 4:30 Thomas began to withdraw, and by 5:30 his men were off the field. The Battle of Chickamauga was over, and it was a Union disaster. But as before, Bragg did not follow up his victory, and the Army of the Cumberland fled into Chattanooga, where it rapidly built up the city's defenses, until it felt safe from attack. Bragg decided to surround the town and starve Rosecrans' troops into surrender; he could do this because of the unusual configuration of the terrain.

Chattanooga rests in a valley with the fast, deep Tennessee River at its north; west of the city the river swings south as far as the base of Lookout Mountain. South of the city Confederates held the mountains. From Lookout Mountain they could control the railroad, the river, and the road; and the besieged Union troops had to depend on supplies coming from the railroad at Stevenson, Alabama, some sixty miles away on the north side of the river. Smith carried a message for Sheridan along this route, going east out of Chattanooga, over the river, up over the long, difficult Walden's Ridge, thence down the Sequatchie valley, through Jasper to Bridgeport. Supplies grew very short in Chattanooga, and the men were on half rations, but great plans were being made, and once again the command setup was revamped.

It was obvious that Bragg's ranking officers had completely lost confidence in him; in fact, President Davis came to the Army of Tennessee to investigate, arriving on October 9. After much discussion, replete with recriminations, charges, and countercharges, Davis decided to retain Bragg in command, but as an aftermath to the Battle of Chickamauga, D. H. Hill was suspended, Polk was sent to Mississippi and Hardee brought to Tennessee to replace him; Forrest was so angry he charged into Bragg's headquarters and threatened to "slap" his jaws. Despite the heavy Union reinforcements coming in to Chattanooga, Bragg materially reduced the strength of his army by sending Longstreet off with his two divisions, and Alexander's artillery and Wheeler's cavalry, to drive Burnside out of east Tennessee; later Buckner was sent with additional troops to aid Longstreet. On the Union side, Thomas replaced Rosecrans; Grant was put in command of a newly formed Division of the Mississippi; Sherman was brought up from Mississippi with two corps, the 15th and 17th; and Major General Joseph Hooker was brought west with the 11th and 12th Corps from the Army of the Potomac.

Grant arrived in Chattanooga on October 23 and wasted no time in getting things moving. First he had to open a supply route: this he did by marching Hooker up the south side of the river from Bridgeport to the base of Lookout Mountain; Brigadier General John B. Turchin's brigade cleared a path to Brown's Ferry, where a bridge was built on pontoons that had been floated down the river, and supplies could be brought in on the route that came to be known as the cracker line. Next Grant proposed to have Sherman take his troops behind the hills on the north side of the river, march them out of sight to the north end of Missionary Ridge, recross the river and attack the ridge. Thomas was to attack to his front and Hooker was to attack Lookout Mountain. On the 23rd Thomas moved forward and captured Orchard Knob, which was used by high-ranking officers as headquarters and an observation post. On the 24th Sherman attacked; he was fooled by the terrain, however, and attacked not Missionary Ridge but a hill near the end of the ridge. Hooker, though, did get up Lookout Mountain in the battle often called "the Battle Above the Clouds." As a matter of fact, there were no clouds, only mist and fog, and the tough fighting took place lower down on the mountain, not at the top. On the 25th Sherman attacked the true north end of Missionary Ridge and had a rough time of it; unable to break the Confederate line, Thomas's men were ordered to advance straight up the ridge and capture the lowest of three lines of rifle pits. This they did, and after a brief halt, fought on up the ridge, an irresistible attack which was made without orders; the Confederate lines broke and their men ran, and Missionary Ridge belonged to the Union. The troops which had held Sherman at bay had to evacuate, and the whole Confederate Army pulled back, first to the Chickamauga and then to Dalton, Georgia. Smith had been with General Sheridan during the runaway assault on Missionary Ridge, and there is evidence which indicates that he was the only member of the staff to go all the way to the top with the General.

The armies would now be inactive until spring of 1864, except for a movement into east Tennessee. In September, Burnside had moved into east Tennessee and his opponent Buckner had been ordered to pull out of east Tennessee and march to a position near Chattanooga; Buckner was then absorbed into Bragg's army. On November 4, Bragg had made the bad mistake of splitting his forces, ordering Longstreet to east Tennessee to drive out Burnside and reclaim the area for the Confederacy. Burnside was able to pull his men back into heavily fortified Knoxville in spite of Longstreet's advance, and when Longstreet finally assaulted the city's defenses at Fort Sanders, he was easily repulsed. After the Chattanooga battles Grant sent Sherman with the 15th Corps and Granger with the 4th to east Tennessee to relieve Burnside. As they drew near, Longstreet left Knoxville and moved east, eventually returning to Lee's army; he was seen no more in the West. Smith went to Knoxville with Sheridan, re-enlisted, and received a furlough.

As an aftermath to the Chattanooga battle, there were again the inevitable changes in command. On December 16 General Joseph E. Johnston replaced Bragg as commander of the Army of Tennessee; Hood, recovered from the loss of a leg at Chicka-mauga, rejoined the army. On the Union side, Grant, on March 12, 1864, was put in charge of all Union forces, and he left for the East to coordinate the actions of all the armies; in a month he would call Sheridan to come East to take over the cavalry of the Army of the Potomac. Sherman was now to command in the West, with Major General John M. Schofield replacing Major General John G. Foster (who had replaced Burnside in east Tennessee), Major General James B. McPherson, and Thomas as his principal subordinates. Sherman had made an abortive campaign east of Vicksburg, Mississippi, in February, and Thomas advanced toward the Confederate position at Rocky Face Ridge near Dalton, Georgia, but fell back when it became apparent how strongly defended the position was. By the time Smith returned from his re-enlistment furlough, Sherman was ready to march on Atlanta.

Sherman's three armies were more than double the size of Johnston's force (although Johnston was reinforced by Polk's troops from Mississippi), but once again the terrain dictated the movements of the army. The Western and Atlantic Railroad from Chattanooga to Atlanta was the Confederate supply line, and the closer their forces were to Atlanta, the easier it was for them to get supplies. If Sherman could get behind the Confederate Army and cut this railroad, or if he could use his superior force to fight a battle in the open, Atlanta would be his. The country Sherman started into was rough indeed, although not so wildly spectacular as the area around Chattanooga. The army moved out on May 4. The plan was to have Thomas and Schofield attract the full attention of the Confederates along Rocky Face Ridge while McPherson slipped around the Confederate left and into their rear at Resaca. This maneuver went well until Resaca was reached, but there the Confederates held up McPherson's army. Sherman therefore sent the whole army around to Resaca. Johnston was not fooled, however, and moved his forces back to Resaca, where he was entrenched and ready to meet Sherman by the 13th. There was hard fighting for two days before Sherman got some troops around the Confederate left flank to Calhoun, on the south side of the Oostenaula River, and Johnston fell back. Obviously Johnston wanted to avoid a pitched battle while he was so badly outnumbered. Every position he occupied in his tactically excellent withdrawal was entrenched, and Sherman was not eager to attack an army hidden behind earthworks. The sparring between the armies continued back to Allatoona, a particularly strong, well-chosen position. There Sherman left the railroad and swung out to the Confederate left and marched south, but when he arrived in the Dallas–New Hope Church area, he found that Johnston had anticipated him and was once more in his way, well dug in. The fighting there was so hard that Sherman pushed out to his left and finally headed back to the railroad, concentrating at Acworth. Johnston had good positions there before Marietta, even though he had to back out of the first one and occupy the second one at Kenesaw Mountain. Lieutenant General Polk was killed by an artillery shell on June 14 at Pine Mountain and his place was assigned to Lieutenant General Alexander P. Stewart. Sherman now abandoned his unspectacular but successful flanking tactics and made a frontal attack on Kenesaw Mountain; the position was invulnerable, and the Union force paid a heavy price in casualties for the rash assault. Having learned a bitter lesson, Sherman sent McPherson around to the right and Johnston had to leave Kenesaw and Marietta. The next Confederate defense line was in front of the Chattahoochee River, and there Sherman went far around to his own left with Schofield, while keeping pressure all along Johnston's line. Schofield got across the river easily and Johnston on July 9 had to fall back to keep Schofield from moving directly into Atlanta; the new Confederate positions were on the south side of Peach Tree Creek.

On the 17th of July, Johnston was informed that he was replaced by General Hood, and the Confederate Army now had a rash, impetuous leader instead of the sagacious, careful "Joe" Johnston. General Benjamin Franklin Cheatham took Hood's old corps, and Stewart and Hardee commanded the other two. Hood planned to attack Thomas when Thomas crossed the Peach Tree Creek, utilizing the usual Sherman tactic, but by the time Stewart and Hardee attacked, Thomas was able to throw them back with substantial losses. McPherson meanwhile was moving on the Confederate right; troops had to be shifted immediately in that direction and the Peach Tree Creek battle ended. Hood then decided to attack McPherson, who was east of Atlanta near Decatur; first he withdrew to the final Atlanta defense line, then sent Hardee to outflank McPherson. On July 22 Hardee struck the Union left a severe blow; his attack came as a great surprise to the Union officers. Casualties were heavy on both sides (McPherson himself was killed), but the attack was repulsed. Major General Oliver O. Howard took over McPherson's army after it was briefly commanded by Major General John A. Logan. By the 22nd Sherman was shelling Atlanta and, using Howard's troops, moving around to the west of the city. At Ezra Church, on July 28, Hood attacked Howard, but the Union men dug in and could not be overwhelmed. Now Sherman's cavalry moved clear around Atlanta to Lovejoy's Station, due south of the city, cutting the Macon and Western Railroad; but they could not hold their position. As usual, those excellent cavalrymen Wheeler and Forrest were tearing things up behind the federal army, as far back as Nashville and Chattanooga. But even their destructive work could not save Atlanta from the persistent Sherman, who sent Schofield around to the west to Rough and Ready, and Howard to Jonesboro. On August 31 Hood ordered Hardee to attack Howard at Jonesboro, but the attack failed. It was clear then even to Hood that he had to get out of Atlanta. Hardee, under heavy fire, moved first, entrenching at Lovejoy's Station. The Confederate troops still in Atlanta then left the city for Hardee's strong position, and Brigadier General Henry W. Slocum's Union forces entered the city from the north.

It is difficult to understand why Sherman did not crush Hood at Lovejoy's Station, but he did not; instead, he moved most of his troops into the city and left Hood in his fortifications. Our Private Smith entered Atlanta with his division and enjoyed a long rest, over to the east of the city. Although Sherman was resting, Hood was not; on September 21 he moved west to Palmetto, and four days later Jefferson Davis visited his army. Again there were command changes, with Hardee sent east and Cheatham taking his place; the corps commanders were now Cheatham, Stewart, and Lieutenant General Stephen D. Lee. General Beauregard was brought back to this theatre, nominally to be Hood's immediate superior. Once again the Confederate cavalry was busy behind Sherman; to protect against them, Sherman sent two divisions to Tennessee: Thomas to Nashville and Schofield to east Tennessee; other troops were sent to Missouri to help subdue the troublesome Price.

When Hood and Beauregard began to move at the end of September of 1864, they moved north, hoping to so interrupt Sherman's supply lines that he would come out of Atlanta and fight; if he did not do so, then Hood would go where Sherman went. When Hood marched back over the same area through which Johnston and Sherman had recently fought, Sherman did come after him. The Confederates gobbled up small units of the Union Army along the railroad, although they did not succeed in capturing Allatoona. They bypassed Rome, and on October 12 were at Resaca. They went through Dalton, finally stopping along the Chickamauga, where the battle had been fought more than a year earlier. Hood then marched west into Alabama to Decatur and Tuscumbia; Sherman abandoned the chase after reaching northern Alabama and turned back to Atlanta, already planning his famous march to the sea. He did send two corps, the 4th and 23rd, to Thomas, before starting for Savannah, confident that Thomas could handle Hood. By now, Private Smith was with his division back in Tennessee, and Thomas and the Army of the Cumberland will be the final focus of our attention.

After crossing the Tennessee at Tuscumbia, Hood went to Florence, then struck out for Columbia, on the Duck River. He was trying to get around Pulaski, Tennessee, where Schofield (in whose army Smith was serving) was located, thus cutting him off from Nashville. Schofield reacted promptly, however, and rushed his army north, beating Hood to Columbia. He fortified the town so that Hood, who was there in strength by November 27, decided not to attack but rather to hold Schofield in place through dummy attacks while he crossed the river above the town, and raced north to Spring Hill, there to cut the road and trap Schofield neatly between two forces. The plan almost worked: the river was crossed, and the Confederates came up to Spring Hill, but for reasons not entirely clear even today the vital road was not blocked. Schofield meanwhile turned his army around and, while the road was still open, passed his troops along the road within sight of the Confederates at Spring Hill and on into the next town north: Franklin. A great Confederate opportunity had been lost. Smith marched safely through Spring Hill and into Franklin with his division.

At Franklin, Schofield put his men behind unusually strong defenses and waited for Hood; he did not have to wait long, for Hood ordered a frontal assault. The Battle of Franklin on November 30 demonstrated the courage of the Confederates, who repeatedly attacked — over open ground and through murderous fire — Union forces that were fully protected by entrenchments. Schofield's army, commanded during the battle by Major General Jacob D. Cox, had positions too strong to be taken. Losses by the Confederates were very high, certainly more than 6,000 dead and wounded. Nevertheless, Schofield pulled his troops out of Franklin and marched them north into strongly fortified Nashville; Hood followed and laid siege to the city.

Nashville rests in a bend of the Cumberland River, and with the river as a barrier to the north, Hood had only to place troops to the southeast, south, and southwest to encircle the city. Since his troops were not sufficient in number to spread them in force throughout this arc, he concentrated them to the south and southeast and bent his open left flank around to the south to provide some slight protection to his main concentration. In the five-mile gap between this bent left flank and the river he relied on one small infantry unit and cavalry patrols. The Union troops in superior numbers were behind the carefully planned, exceedingly strong defenses of the city; Thomas meanwhile was preparing to attack Hood as soon as his cavalry was ready. But his superiors in the East wanted him to attack without delay; Grant, reflecting the wishes of Stanton and Lincoln, ordered him to attack at once. Thomas replied that as soon as he could get horses for his cavalry, he would advance. His inactivity was misinterpreted as procrastination — or worse — and

Grant ordered him replaced, only to delay the order when he learned that freezing rain on December 8-9 made all movement impossible. A few days later Grant ordered Major General John A. Logan of Illinois to go to Nashville and take command, but he soon decided the situation needed his personal attention and he left Virginia for Tennessee. There is some evidence that Schofield was scheming to get Thomas's job, but before a change of any kind could be made, the ice melted and on December 15, Thomas attacked. His plan was simple: an attack on the Confederate right (southeast) and a major attack into the open Confederate left flank to the west. On the 15th the attack on the right did not make much headway; but on the left the outnumbered Confederates had to give way, and the Union troops were rolling through the Confederate line as darkness fell. Hood did not retreat that night, although he did move back a short distance and form a new line. On the 16th Thomas repeated his pattern of attack, and the result was a complete Union victory; what was left of Hood's army retreated back through Franklin to Columbia, where Forrest's cavalry joined them and effectively screened the rest of the retreat. Forrest had been ordered by Hood to Murfreesboro and had won a battle outside that town on December 7, but he could not pierce its defenses and effect its capture. The Confederates kept going south, pursued by the cavalry of Major General James H. Wilson as far as the Tennessee River. After this retreat the Army of Tennessee was no longer a major factor in the war.

Benjamin T. Smith was in the pursuit of Hood to the Tennessee River, and this was his last exposure to enemy action. Although he would remain in the army for almost another year, his duty would be in the army of occupation—when he was not on furlough. Altogether, Smith was a good soldier who did his job with intelligence and application. His contribution to the Northern war effort was not particularly outstanding, but multiplied by a million, Smith's army service makes it easier for us to understand how the Union was preserved.

CLYDE C. WALTON

March 4, 1963

A BIBLIOGRAPHICAL NOTE

THE Benjamin T. Smith journal is written on 232 lined pages of a book which measures eight by eleven inches; it is one of more than 250,000 Civil War manuscripts in the Illinois State Historical Library. Many of these manuscripts were presented to the Library and the people of Illinois by their owners; the Smith journal was the gift of Smith's grand-nephew, Mr. Joseph R. Wood.

Smith's handwriting is quite legible, and the original journal is easy to read. But if Smith's letters are clearly formed, his sentences and paragraphs are not. He was addicted to interminably long sentences —sentences that were often a page in length—and each sentence was heavily punctuated with commas. Although he did not intend to obfuscate meaning, his inevitable habit of capitalizing the letters "A" and "S," when these began a word, certainly does so. And his spelling, while not particularly bad, was not good enough for him to be the last one standing at an old-fashioned spell-down.

There is internal evidence sufficient to demonstrate that the manuscript was written after the war ended. From beginning to end, the writing is in the same ink and uniform in style. The writing and the paper itself (which is bright and smooth) show none

of the marks of hard campaigning—the unmistak-
able evidence of rain and snow, the cramped entries
written by flickering camp fire, the wear and tear of
a book carried for years in a soldier's pack. Almost
all of the surviving diaries and journals actually kept
in the field during the war are of the pocket-size variety, measuring generally either 3″ x 5″ or 4″ x 6″;
this journal is written in the much more unwieldy
8″ x 11″.

One suspects that Smith kept one or more of
smaller journals during the war, beginning probably
when he arrived at Camp Douglas, and at war's end
recopied these journals into the Library's volume.
Very little hindsight in the way of postwar remi-
niscence has crept into this manuscript; Smith's entry for Spring Hill, as an example, could have been
written a day or two after the event when he was
safe in Nashville and realized how narrow an escape
the Union Army had experienced. This entry could
have been written after the war, but if it was, Smith
ignored what must have been an overpowering urge
to expand upon the Union escape at Spring Hill.
Then, too, Smith resists the temptation to make himself occupy a larger role than he actually filled; he
does not try to make himself something that he
never was.

All in all, Smith's manuscript seems to have been
copied into its present form from a day by day diary-
journal kept during the war. It seems logical to as-

sume that this manuscript was copied shortly after the war was over. And, finally, it is a matter of equal logic that very little was added to the manuscript when it was copied.

The manuscript as published here is generally as Smith wrote it, except that a number of his longer sentences have been broken up or repunctuated when it seemed necessary for ease of reading or to make Smith's meaning clear. His persistent capitalization of "A" and "S" has not been followed; periods have been added to his abbreviations as in "bro."; where placenames are misspelled, correct spellings have been inserted in brackets; at the first occurrence of the name of an officer important to the narrative, his first name and middle initial have been supplied in brackets. Other than these additions and small changes, the manuscript is as Smith wrote it.

I acknowledge with thanks the assistance of Clarkson A. Collins III, Librarian, Rhode Island Historical Society; David Jonah, Director of Libraries, Brown University; Mrs. Lenore Harrington, Reference Librarian, Missouri Historical Society; and the National Archives. Particularly am I grateful for the resourcefulness of Miss Margaret A. Flint of the Illinois State Historical Library in answering my questions; of Mrs. Ellen Whitney of the Illinois State Historical Library for her tireless pursuit of essential detail; of Mrs. Helene Levene of the Civil War Centennial Commission of Illinois for her re-

search into the history of the 51st Illinois; and to
Mrs. Norma J. Darovec of the Illinois State Historical Library for her patient and careful typing of the
manuscript.

A special word of thanks goes to my good friend
E. B. "Pete" Long for his valuable assistance, and
to his wife, Barbara, who drew the excellent maps
which accompany the text of the journal.

CLYDE C. WALTON

Springfield, Illinois
March 4, 1963

Private Smith's Journal

Recollections of the Late War

By B. T. Smith

CHAPTER I

Wherein Benjamin T. Smith, an 18-year-old Illinois farmhand and general laborer, bored with his life, decides to join the army. After a hazardous freight train ride to Kankakee, Illinois, to visit his mother, he enlists on October 8, 1861. He trains in his own unusual way for army life and soon is sent to Camp Douglas in Chicago, where he is mustered into Company C, 51st Illinois Volunteer Infantry. The monotony of training is broken by a recruiting trip to Kankakee; he then serves as assistant camp postmaster; observes a riot in camp, grieves over a friend's untimely death, and goes again to Kankakee to recruit, this time enlisting, among others, his brother Calvin. After being promoted camp postmaster he resigns the position so he can go south to fight with his regiment.

1861 In the year of our Lord, just as the summer months are nearly spent, and the fall is about to come, and paint the forest leaves, in their various tints and shades, I find my self domesticated with

3

Bro. Joe, and his partner Jonas, at a small Hamlet called Watseka in Illinois. We were engaged in building a two story frame house, or rather they were, while I was helping to the best of my poor ability. Our home is at Kankakee, a thriving town some thirty five miles away, wherein we left our Mother, Bros. Cal as we called him for short, and Walter the youngest with Julia the next oldest, of the family group after Walter. It was a scorching hot summer just past and I had worked a part of the time in the harvest field near by, work not altogether congenial to my taste, I must confess. Harvest being over, my time is occupied with the building, which is under roof, but without doors or windows as yet. After supper each evening, I manage to get hold of some paper or other and scan its columns for the daily budget of war news. One evening, the paper had a full account of the first battle of the war, and I read, with a good deal of interest, all about the details of the engagement, and how our boys in blue scampered off the field stampeded by the rebels; how some of them did not stop their flight until they reached Washington. Heretofore it had not entered my head that I might don the blue, myself, but this news from the front, fired my boyish feelings, and upon reading further on, that the President had issued a call for three hundred thousand men[1], I

[1]This statement of Smith's is puzzling because President Lincoln's proclamation calling for 300,000 troops was not issued until July 1, 1862. The first call for troops (on April

made up my mind to enlist, A company I learn is organizing, over at the county seat about a mile from here. Tomorrow I will go over and see if they have any use for a boy of seventeen. At bed time we go aloft to the upper regions where we sleep, since the roof has been finished, and, after the sputtering candle has been carefully extinguished, and we have got into our respective positions for sleep, I begin to rack my brain as to the best way in which to approach the subject, which is agitating my mind, to Joe, who is in a manner the head of the family. After much thinking over many plans to throw out some hints by way of feelers, and when Joe is about to drop off into the embrace of morpheus, I bring his senses back to mundane things by saying, Joe!! I am going for a "sojer." Without giving him time to dijest this piece of news, I continue; I am going over to Old-town tomorrow and enlist. Then I subsided. Oh are we? said he, and ha! ha! ho- ho- he laughed. You'd make a fine soldier wouldent you? And he turned over with a bounce and went to sleep, while Jonas snored in unison, and I lay awake thinking of the matter for hours. He might look at it as a joke, but it was no joke to me, as I would show him. I could see our boys in my mind as they scattered helter

---

15, 1861) was for a total of 75,000 militia; the second call (on May 3, 1861) was for 42,034 volunteers for three years of service, for 22,714 regulars and 18,000 seamen. Perhaps Smith confuses Lincoln's call for 300,000 men with the action of Congress, on July 22, 1861, authorizing an army with a strength of 500,000.

skelter off the field of Bulls Run, and the old saw
ran through my mind.

> He who fights, and runs away
> May live to fight another day.
> And the Kings men marched up the hill
> And then marched down again,
> As they did at Bunker Hill.

Then I thought of my younger days, when I was
a young shaver, in Providence when there was two
factions among us school boys. How often we met
down near the head of the Basin[2] and armed with
clods and turfs would engage in a battle royal charging each other until our ammunition was exhausted,
then retire to load up again. Some of us would get a
black eye or bloody nose now and then, which we
did not mind much. We are up with the sun, and as
Joe seems to ignore the subject of last nights an-
nouncement, I told him I was going home to see
Mother. I spent the day as usual, and after night had
set in, a freight train came along, bound for Gilman.
Joe and Jonas helped me into an empty box car,
with a big satchel stuffed full of clothes to be taken
home for the wash. I hadent bargained for this, and
it was a big load to carry as well, but I threw it in a
corner and sat down on it as the train started. I had
five dollars in my pocket which I had earned, but
concluded to hold on to it, if I could get through

---

[2] A body of water formed by the confluence of the Woona-
squatucket and Moshassuck rivers, called Providence Cove;
in Smith's youth it was enclosed in a circular basin.

without using it. I reached Gilman about eleven o'clock; here it was necessary to change on to the Ill. Central, so I got out on the dark side of the train, and found it was sleeting and freezing, which made things awful slippery under foot, and the night was as dark as Egypt. I waited around until a freight came along going my way, and just as it was pulling out I placed the satchel on a narrow projection of one of the cars and left it there, while I went up the side of the car by the foot holds like a squirrel. I found the tops of the cars covered with the fast falling rain which froze as it fell, making them as slippery as glass. The night being so bad was a fortunate circumstance perhaps, as it drove all the breakmen back into the caboose, to warm their shins around the stove. I went over the tops of several cars using a great deal of caution, as was necessary under the circumstances, until I found a car with an end door open, a small square opening big enough to get through. Then I went back to where I had left the satchel, and while the train was then fully under way, going at least fifteen miles an hour, I climbed down the side and got my grip, took it to the top of the car, and forward again to the car with the end opening; crawling through I dropped on the top of some barrels of flour with which the car was loaded. I was all tired out with the exertion I had made, and was glad of a rest. And then I had time to reflect on the foolhardy thing I had done, and vow I wouldn't go through such a thing again.

About five o'clock in the morning the train crossed the bridge over the Kankakee river and slowed up; taking advantage of this, I clambered out, and off the train and struck a bee line for home. But I took care to say nothing of my mode of travel to any one. I spent two days at home, and having secured a reluctant consent from Mother, returned to Watseka, this time by the regular mode of travel, by passenger train.

Oct 8th Reach here early this morning. During the day I put in the time around the house. After supper I walk over to the Court House, and find quite a concourse of the people of the town gathered around the court room. I listen to a speech then going on, the speaker calling for volunteers to come up and join the company being formed. I went up to the table surrounded by busy signers and at the first chance that offered put my name on the roll. When all those present that wished to had signed, the roll was called, and some sixty odd answered. Then a motion was made to elect officers. It was carried. Mr N B Petts was elected Captain, a Mr Tilton[3] 1st

---

[3] These two men are Nathaniel B. Petts, a 27-year-old nurseryman from Middleport, Illinois, and Albert M. Tilton, a 26-year-old railroad agent from the same city. So that the reader will not be interrupted constantly by identifications of individuals whose presence was not a major factor in Smith's army career, only those whose identification is necessary to a further understanding of the narrative will be identified in footnotes. All of Smith's friends in the 51st Illinois can be identified through the surviving muster rolls in the Illinois State Archives.

Lieutenant. It being late we were dismissed, to reconvene at the call of the Capt. I started for home with regular military step, chin up, chest forward, as suited the importance of the occasion. Joe and Jonas had gone to bed. Instead of turning in myself I concluded to take a quilt, and deposit my would be military form on the hard floor, and thus go into training for future emergencies. The first half hour I spent in running over in my mind, the probable features of what my future experience would be. I had mentally got through the first day's march, with sore feet and tired limbs, when it dawned in upon me that the floor was not quite as soft a bed as the one I usually occupied. The side I lay on was kicking to be relieved, so I turned over and gave the other side a chance, in fact I changed sides frequently for the next hour or two, first one side, then the other; then I tried my back with no better success. I soon felt as though I had been pounded all over, and concluded to give it up as a bad job, so I crawled into bed, as carefully as I could, so as not to disturb the sleepers. But I had only just got settled with a sigh of great relief, when a couple of giggles, followed by a loud laugh from both of them, and a voice spake in the darkness, saying wont you make a fine soldier, and a lot of chaff in the same strain. I maintained a dignified silence. In fact I was like the darkey that was caught stealing a chicken, had nothing to say. So the chaffing fell flat, as I continued to keep mum.

9th I was up bright and early. Feeling none the worse for my last nights experience so I made up my mind to try it again, as we can get used to any thing, if well persisted in, so I have heard. Word came that we will meet tomorrow. I am pleased at this, as I am anxious to be off.

Oct 10th Last night I had little or no trouble with my bed on the floor; its true I used a comfort instead of a quilt, which had the advantage of being a trifle thicker. If any body lay awake to get the laugh on me, they must have been some what disappointed, for I slept like a top. At sunrise I was up, and busy with breakfast. At about 11 o'clock I walk over to the Old Town[4], and find the boys all on hand. We form in line and are sized up, with the tallest on the right; my five feet, seven and a half inches, brings me a little to the right of the center of the line. Counting off by two's, we right face, and march to New town (Watseka) passing near our house. I looked neither to the right or left but from the corner of my eye, I see Joe and Jonas watching us file by. Reaching the Stanley House, we break ranks and go in to dinner, which proves to be quite a fine

[4]"Old Town" was Middleport, Illinois; "New town" was south Middleport. In 1861 Middleport was the county seat of Iroquois County; on September 17, 1863, south Middleport was renamed Watseka. A legislative act approved February 7, 1865, removed the county seat to Watseka, where it has since remained. Although legally there was no Watseka in 1861, doubtless the name was then in common use in the area.

spread, ending up with ice cream, which sets me to wondering, if we will get any ice cream down in Dixie. We may get a chill or two, not flavored with strawberry however. After dinner we march to the train waiting for us in which we are to be transported to Chicago. The towns people all turn out to see us off. Among them are Mothers, Fathers, sisters and brothers to many of the members of our company. The bell rings, and the train starts slowly along, while the people cheered and waved their hands and handkerchiefs; some of them are in tears, and no doubt send a silent prayer after us, hoping we may return, when the war is over. How many of our cheerful band indeed will return. No one can tell what the fates may have in store for us. We heed not what tomorrow may bring forth, as we move cheerfully along on our way.

We arrive in Chicago at 9:30 P.M. March to the Lloyd House where supper is awaiting us, to which we do full justice. After our meal, we march to the old Republican WigWam[5]. Army blankets, one to each of us, was issued, most of us paired off into couples, spreading one blanket on the floor, and the other over us. Charley Miller and I bunk down to-

[5]The Wigwam was a wooden building, 180' by 100', located on the southeast corner of present Lake Street and Wacker Drive in Chicago. It cost between $5,000 and $6,000 and was built to house the Republican Convention of 1860— the convention that nominated Lincoln for President. In 1861 the building was sold for $950 and converted to commercial use; it was destroyed by fire after the Civil War ended.

gether. I soon learn he has been a clerk in a drug store. Also by the frequency with which he changes his position, that he lacks the *veteran* experience I have had, with the floor for a bed. Said experience, though limited to a couple of nights, stands me in good stead.

11th I woke up at day break, and find many of the boys, with their blankets wrapped around them, trying to snatch a wink of sleep, in a sitting position, braced up in a corner or against the wall, after the terrors of an unyielding floor. After a wash up all round, with tin basins and towels, furnished by some kindly souls for our use, marched to the Lloyd House again for breakfast, after which, we boarded some street cars, which convey us to Camp Douglass[6], out in the suburbs on Cottage Grove Ave. Here we find a large tract of ground enclosed by a high fence and long lines of barracks newly constructed; we took possession of one which we find clean and comfortable. Two story bunks are arranged along one side, each built double, for two to occupy. In the rear of each company quarters is a kitchen with a long table and benches for one hundred men. After Roll call, we are assigned as Co "C" 51st Ill "Vol". The 51st is one of four regiments, which is to comprise the Douglass Brigade; the other three are the 22d 27th and 42d. Ill Regiments.

[6]The best study of Camp Douglas is by Joseph L. Eisendrath, "Chicago's Camp Douglas, 1861–1865," in the *Journal of the Illinois State Historical Society*, Volume 53, Number 1 (Spring, 1960), pages 37–63.

I learn that our name as the Douglass brigade is given us by Stephen A Douglass, who after his defeat by Abe Lincoln for the Presidency, turned his patriotic energies to raising troops, for the army.

Oct 12th Last night, our first in camp, I was put on guard duty, with a stick in lieu of a gun. For two hours I tramp along my beat with deliberate circumspection, but the time seemed mortal long before I was relieved, and allowed to turn in for four hours sleep. Then two more hours tramping again.

Charley Miller and I become chums, and bunk mates. He is a year or so older than myself, and seems to be a boy of good morals, so we become firm friends at once.

13th The Company march over to the Quarter Masters quarters, and each is supplied with a uniform. Returning, we doff our civilian suits, and put on the blue, and discover a grotesque lot of misfits. Our good Quarter Master must have had a mistaken idea that he was clothing a company of giants; we rolled the pants up at the bottom and lapped them over at the top, and still the legs looked like a collapsed balloon.

We were told that was the best he could do for the present, until another supply came, when an exchange for better fits would be furnished; with this we had to be content.

Oct 22d Our days are spent in routine duties, with drilling by squads, companies, Battalions and regimental, also the manual of arms, some old mus-

Civil War Awkward Squad

kets being furnished for that purpose. I with a few others are learning the broad sword exercise, using ash sticks with basket hilts, and are taught by Sergt. Exstrand [John H. E. Kestrand], who has served seven years in the Swedish Army.

Capt. Petts asked me this morning if I thought I could get any recruits in my home town Kankakee. I answered yes.

Report to me about 5 P.M. I did so and was given a weeks furlough, and transportation for myself and any number of men I might return with. I arrive at home about 10:30 P.M. and find them all well except Mother who is not feeling altogether well.

Oct 28 I am again in camp, having secured from among my old school mates, eight recruits, whom I turned over to the Captain, who expressed him self as well pleased. I am detailed by Col [Joseph K.] Tucker Commander of the Post, as assistant Post Master of the Camp. Wm Monroe is P.M. There are

some twelve to fifteen thousand troops within the
Camp, so the semi daily mails are of considerable
importance. Mother, Julia and Walter, are to arive
this evening on their way East; after supper I hasten
down town again, and go to the Lake Shore Depot
and find them on the train and stay with them until
the train starts. Then bidding them good by, return
to Camp. Bro. Cal is still in KKK.

Oct 29th The building used as the Post Office is
separate from any of the others, and fitted up for
exclusive mail purposes. I enter upon my duties at
once, which are to carry the mail to the office down
town and return with the mail for camp. Both morning and evening, a crowd of expectants await around
the delivery window until the mail is destributed,
into their several initial pigeon holes, and then delivered to their several owners.

Dec 23 The orderly condition of our camp has
continued for the past two months; only once during that time has the peace and unity been disturbed. A Regiment of Sappers and miners, partially
organized, was ordered to disband. A number of the
men enlisted in other regiments, but some of them
while unassigned, smuggled a lot of whiskey into
camp, and getting uncomfortably full, about 9:30
P.M. got into a row with some of the members of the
45th Lead Mine Boys[7], and very soon a small sized

[7]Camp Douglas was then full of small companies of men,
as yet unassigned to regiments. The state government was
doing its best to form regiments from these companies, but

riot commenced. Sticks as well as fists were freely used, some of them taking advantage of the row, attacked the sutler store, and cleaned out the whole stock, and ended by pulling the building to pieces. Col Tucker[8] buckled on his sword and called out our regiment to suppress the riot, which was done in short order. The Col however was pretty roughly handled, but escaped with some scratches and a torn uniform. The Guard house was filled with the rioters that were arrested. The Col. belongs to the

---

organization proceeded slowly. The 45th Regiment of Illinois Volunteer Infantry had been raised in the far northwestern corner of Illinois, where lead mining was a major industry. The *Chicago Tribune* of December 24, 1861, reported a different version of this disturbance:

Rumored Affray at Camp Douglas

There were rumors in the city yesterday that on Sunday night, while attempting to break out of the guard house, three soldiers had been wounded, one of them severly. As near as we could learn, the men pulled off a board from the side of the building, and obtained possession of some muskets belonging to the sentry. Thus armed, the prisoners became turbulent and made known their intention of leaving their uncomfortable quarters. In using the force necessary to prevent this, three of the contestants received ugly wounds from sabre-bayonets. We give this as the general terror of the story spread about the streets yesterday, trusting that it may upon examination prove without proper foundation in fact.

[8]Colonel Joseph H. Tucker was not a regular army officer. He was appointed by Governor Yates in 1861 to command the northern district of Illinois and to construct barracks to house newly recruited soldiers. He left Camp Douglas in February, 1862, but returned in June, 1862, as commander of the 69th Illinois Infantry and of Camp Douglas, and ran the camp until January, 1863.

regular army, and is an officer of determination and strict discipline and very dressy. It must have taken him some time to recover his "infra dig."

Jany 18th 1862 My chum Charley Miller, who was sent to the Post Hospital a few days ago, having caught a severe cold, which developed into a raging fever died last night[9] unexpectedly, which caused me much sorrow, as we had become very much attached to each other. The funeral took place this afternoon, he was buried with military honors, a salute being fired over his grave, and the regimental band playing a dead march. He is the first member from our company to cross the line over into the great beyond.

Jany 22d I am again sent on recruiting service to Kankakee. Mrs. Sutcliffe and Will insisted upon my staying with them while in town. Skirmishing around among the boys I secure a batch of recruits, and as Calvin[10] wants to go too He is taken with the rest.

28th We all return to Camp, my papers furnishing transportation for the lot. I turn them all over to Capt Petts, and find that during my absence, Monroe the P.M. has resigned, and I am promoted in his place.

[9]Charles W. Miller was a 20-year-old clerk from Middleport, Illinois, who died of pneumonia at Camp Douglas on January 7, 1862, according to the muster roll in Illinois State Archives.

[10]Calvin R. Smith, according to the muster roll in the Illinois State Archives, was enlisted in Chicago on February 8, 1861. He is described as 5 feet 8 inches tall, with brown hair and dark eyes, being by profession a "painter."

Feb 12th News came that Genl [Ulysses S.] Grant is besieging Ft Donaldson [Donelson], on the Tenn.[11] River, and our brigade is to join him at once. Our regiment has only eight companies, and is only 600 strong, 400 short of a full compliment. I tender my resignation as P.M. Col. Tucker informed me, my services had proved very satisfactory, and he would make my detail permanent if I wished to stay. I respectfully declined, as I had not enlisted for that purpose, so I rejoined my Company.

[11] Fort Donelson is on the Cumberland, not the Tennessee River.

Chapter II

Wherein Benjamin T. Smith and the 51st Illinois arrive in Cairo, February 15, 1862, and here receive additional training and equipment. Smith and the 51st march to New Madrid, Missouri, but participate only in a demonstration; they then pursue the troops that have evacuated Island Number 10, in the Mississippi River, eventually capturing some of them near Tiptonville, Tennessee. The regiment arrives at Shiloh too late to enter the battle, but takes part in the slow advance towards Corinth, Mississippi. Here Smith participates in a series of inconclusive skirmishes prior to the city's evacuation. On July 21 the regiment leaves Corinth and marches south and east into northern Alabama, where a peaceful month is spent guarding the Memphis and Charleston Railroad near Decatur. When Confederate General Braxton Bragg moves north on his "invasion" of Kentucky, Smith and the 51st Illinois are a part of the Union force sent to help get him out of that state.

Feby 14th We are enroute for Cairo Ill. Arriving on the 15th and go into barracks to await for our equipments. Guns and ammunition are issued to us. It is the old Belgium musket[1]. They are a heavy un-

[1]General Ulysses S. Grant described these imported weapons as being "almost as dangerous to the person firing it as the one aimed at."

Wharf-boat at Cairo, Illinois

gainly looking arm, and we are not at all pleased with them.

16th A squad of our company under Sergt [Ivan L.] Bailey go out on the flats back of town to try our guns, target shooting. We gave them a fair trial, but found them wanting. After a few rounds, they choked up so badly that it was impossible to shoot straight, and they kicked like the business end of a mule. Going back to quarters, we reported results, and the regiment decided they did not want them. When we were called out at 5:30 P.M. for the usual dress parade, drawn up in line behind the row of stacked guns, when the order came from the Adjutant to take arms. Not a hand moved. Thinking the order was not understood, it was repeated, with a like result. So there was meeting in Camp, the line officers were called up, explanations followed. After the officers returned to their respective places in the ranks, the Adjutant ([Charles W.] Davis) said the orders would have to be obeyed, or another armed regiment would confront us and compel us, so he repeated again the order, but no heed was taken of it, and so we were ordered back to barracks, and the guns remained in stack. Better arms were promised us next day.

17th It has rained all night and the guns have remained out so most of them are full of water. New arms were issued today. The Harpers Ferry musket[2], rifled, a much lighter and neater gun, with which we are better pleased.

News came that Ft. Donaldson has surrendered to Grant so we will not be obliged to go there, 'tis said that several thousand prisoners fell into his hands.

Feb 27th To day is my birth day, but nothing is being done to celebrate the august event, no banquet is spread, so I make the most of it by feasting on hard tack and sowbelly. Well I am eighteen, and that is not to be sneezed at.

The past ten days have gone quickly enough, filled in with drilling, practice at shooting at a mark, until I have become quite expert. Orders have just come to be ready in marching order in ten minutes; our knapsacks are packed, equipments in order and we are in line before the ten minutes have expired.

---

[2]This was a rifle musket, made at the U.S. Arsenal at Harper's Ferry; it was a .58 caliber weapon, first perfected in 1855, and it was in common use during the war.

Marching down on the levee we board a steamboat which conveys us over the Ohio river and we land upon Kentucky soil; our tents accompany us and are soon erected in company line, and we are experiencing camp life for the first time.

March 2d A good deal of rain has fallen in the past few days, consequently the Ohio is slowly but surely rising; and will inundate our camp, orders issued to strike tents. A steamboat is ready to convey us, and our worldly effects, across the Mississippi and we land at Birds Point, and start on a march into the interior. At night fall we reach Bertran [Bertrand] and go into camp, tired and hungry, and turn in to rest on the hard ground, after this our first days' march.

Our surgeon told us that when on a march a stop is made for rest, to lay on our backs and in that position we would get more rested in three minutes, then ten in any other position, which proved to be the case.

Mch 3d We have marched all day, and go into camp- while the rain is coming down in torrents, a bunch of us find a barn, and get under its friendly shelter. It is pitch dark and we are soaked through, but we find some hay from which we drive some stray pigs, who resent our intrusion with grunts of dissatisfaction, to which we pay not the slightest heed, but dump our miserable frames on the hay and I am asleep in no time.

Mch 4th We are up at day break, I am feeling none

1862 In The West

the worse from sleeping in my wet clothes, get a fire going and soon have a tin cup of streaming hot coffee, minus the sugar or milk, but it tastes like nectar just the same. Have marched all day. and go into camp in front of New Madrid[3]. Near here is where the great earth quake of 1811[4] took place, the ground for acres around sinking, some fifty feet, the effect of which is still plainly to be seen. Our camp is laid out and tents erected; our canvas houses are called the Sibley tent, and is shaped like an indian tepee, circular in form, running to a point at the top, and capable of holding eight or ten men, sleeping with their feet towards the center pole, the lower end of the pole ends in an iron tri pod, so that a fire can be built in the center.

Maj. Genl Jno Pope is our corps commander

[3] Smith loses track of his time here, skipping the month of April. The 51st Illinois was assigned on March 10 to Paine's Division; on the 14th of March New Madrid was evacuated. It was on April 8–9, not March, that the Confederates surrendered near Tiptonville, Tennessee; it was the 11–12 of April that the troops moved to Ft. Pillow. It was April 21–22, not March 21–22, when the Regiment reached the Shiloh battlefield, and of course the action around Farmington took place at the end of April, not March. Beginning with the May 9 entry, Smith is again right with time.

[4] The first shocks of one of the greatest earthquakes ever recorded occurred on November 16, 1811, and were centered on New Madrid, Missouri. Some thirty thousand square miles were affected, sinking as much as fifteen feet; the course of the Mississippi River was changed in several places, and the "American Bottom" area of Illinois experienced severe damage.

and Brig Genl [Eleazer A. Paine] Payne commands our Brigade[5].

Our Colonel (Cummings [Gilbert W. Cumming]) is not with us, so the regiment is in charge of Lt Col Bradley (L[uther] P.). Some miles east of us is Island #10 in the Miss. River, and is fortified and held by the rebels. Adml. Porter is besieging it with a fleet of mortar boats; we can hear the reports of each mortar as it is fired, and in the darkness, we can see the fuse of the shells, as they circle above the tree tops, and hear them explode.

Mch 6th our brigade is ordered out, and march down in the vicinity of the town which is held by the rebels who are well fortified, besides two of their gun boats are in the river. We have two enormous siege guns down in the swamp, which are pounding away at the fort and town; we have also some of Berdans sharp shooters, armed with telescop rifles, & posted in the tops of some tall trees, aiming to pick off any of the enemy that come within range. We are drawn-up in line, and ordered to load our guns, our ammunition consists of three buck shot and a ball, which

[5]The Union Army at New Madrid and Island No. 10 was led by Major General John Pope. The 51st Illinois was commanded by Lieutenant Colonel Luther P. Bradley, since Colonel Gilbert W. Cumming was leading the 2nd Brigade of Brigadier General Eleazer A. Paine's 4th Division. Admiral Porter was not at Island No. 10; the naval forces were commanded by Flag Officer Andrew H. Foote. The sharpshooters were not those of Colonel Hiram Berdan, but a special group from the 64th Illinois Infantry, led by Major F. W. Matteson.

would prove very effective at close range. We are cautioned not to fire until ordered, and then to load and fire at will. Getting into a closer position, we draw the fire from one of the gunboats, they had our range, but the gun was aimed to low, so the shot buried itself in the ground, twenty feet in our front. Then we were ordered to lay down, and just in time to escape the next shot which went whizzing just above us. One of their shots aimed at our siege battery, hit one of the guns on the side of its muzzle, and knocked out a big chunk a foot long. From our position we can see how well the town is fortified. High earth works all around it, with a wide deep ditch, full of water, and out side of that, is piled small trees ten feet high with their limbs all sharpened to points and facing outward. We contemplate all this with a good deal of apprehension, if we should be ordered to charge it, and do not feel over confident as to the results.

All ready the rebs are pegging away at us, as the bullets whiz with a sharp hiss over our prostrate position. The order to retire beyond range, is a welcome one, and we march back to camp, and learn that this was only a demonstration to try us under fire. This being our first experience gave us a queer feeling, to state a fact.

Mch 7th we march out by companies to fire the loads from our guns, and it is discovered that two or three of the boys had put their ball down first and the powder on top; needless to say this would have

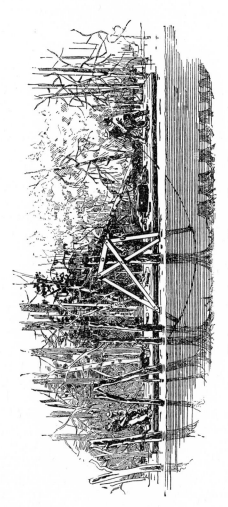

Underwater Sawing to Deepen Channel

made their guns useless for firing. They were guied by the rest of us and reprimanded by the Captain.

Returning to Camp it is learned that New Madrid was evacuated during the night, also Island #10, so our demonstration had some effect; we learn also that a stiff piece of engineering work had been all but accomplished by our sappers and miners. The over flow of the river, extended some miles back into a bayou which was covered with a thick growth of timber. A flat bottom steamer was steamed up to the timber line above the island, a machine was rigged up at its bow, and the trees were cut low enough under the water to enable it (the boat) to float above the stumps, and a pathway was thus made for the passage of our boats around the island; but the timely evacuation of the enemy made it unnecessary to finish the job. One of our gun boats, during the dark night stole its way by the island, without attracting the enemys attention. The retreating rebels are expected to join forces, and move southward; orders to strike tents at once, but almost immediately counter manded, with orders to march leaving the tents standing. Getting into light marching order, carrying only a blanket, and of course arms and rations, we are soon on our way, and reach Point Pleasant on the river at dusk. Owing to the position occupied by the brigade, our regiment line up in a corn field. The soil is soft and muddy owing to the recent rains; here we are expected to stay all night, so we look about us for means to make it possible to

Every Rail a "Top Rail"

rest and sleep without standing in the soft soil ankle deep. Espying a rail fence, we make a raid upon it, but are told we could take only the top rail; well we needed them all, so as fast as the top rail was re-moved the next one was then the top one, so we continued to take the top one until there was no fence left. By this means we managed to secure enough to keep us out of the mud; by laying a number of them one way and each man laying two rails close together, one end on the pile, the lower end in the mud, by careful management I lay on this narrow bed and slept the night through without a motion. The least movement to either side would tumble me into the mud. One may do most any thing by trying hard enough.

Mch 8th our regiment and the 42d embark on a steamboat, the 22d & 27th follow on another. We lay out in mid-stream, while just below is one of our gun boats pounding away at a shore battery, which must be silenced before our boats can pass down the river. The fire from our gun boat is very rapid, and soon the rebels spike their guns and retreat, thus leaving the way open for our advance. We are landed below the rebel fort and start on a march eastward; taking a quick route step, our mission is to intercept the retreat of the rebel forces that recently occupied Island #10 and New Madrid. There is a big bend in the river making a curve of about seventy miles, while across country the two points meet within fifteen miles. The boats had conveyed us to the nearest point across this neck. So while the enemy had a day the start of us, the distance they would have to march, would enable us to head them off, so there was a prospect that we would have a brush with them before another day would end. Passing through Tiptonville Tenn, we continue our rapid

Building Union River Gunboats

march until about 10 P.M. when we come up with the enemy, who are located in some thick timber. The 22d and 27th march around them and take position along the river, while our two regiments lay down in line along the main road. It is a clear frosty night. I lay on my back without undoing my blanket, only cover my throat, and immediately fall fast asleep, as did every body else that could, nor did I awake until just before day. When we were silently aroused, I felt as warm and comfortable as though I had slept upon a bed, but some of the boys were shaking with chills; we marched through the woods and joined the rest of the command. We found all the rebel guns corded up between the trees, and then we knew the enemy has surrendered during the night; forming a half hollow square, we stood on our arms, while the prisoners marched in with Genl. Stevens[6] at their head. Our whole force there present did not exceed 2,600 men while the prisoners numbered over 5,000. Genl. Stevens supposed our whole force

[6] Smith is confused here about the general officer who surrendered at Tiptonville; the officer was Major General William W. Mackall, not Stevens, (Brigadier General Edward W. Gantt also surrendered at Tiptonville). General Paine's report of the expedition to Tiptonville states that on the 8th ". . . was surrendered about 3,900 men, besides the prisoners taken the day before and straggling parties picked up by scouts. The whole force captured exceeded 5,000 men." See: *War of the Rebellion: A Compilation of the Official Records of the Union and Confederate Armies* (Washington: 1880–1901), Series I, Volume 8, pages 109–13. Hereafter cited as *O.R.*, followed by the series and volume numbers, part number (if any), and the page reference.

was on hand some 16,000, but our rapid march had left the rest of our troops a few hours behind us; having only two boats to convey them across the river it took many hours to land them all. If Stevens had been aware of this, he no doubt would not have surrendered without firing a shot.

However we were entirely satisfied with the turn the affair had taken, enabling us to obtain a bloodless victory. About 11 o'clock A.M. our forces came up, and relived us, and we set to at once to get something to eat. The boats have come, and they transport us back to New Madrid, and again we are in camp, a very short but also a very successfull Campaign. We feel much elated at our safe return, from that we expected would be a fight at least of serious dimensions.

Mch 12th Strike tents, three days rations are issued, our ammunition inspected to see if each man has fourty rounds. March to the river and go on board the steamer Genl Taylor. There are a dozen or more steam boats in the fleet, which is to convey our whole corps down the river to Ft Pillow[7], which is being besieged by our fleet of gun boats, and mortar boats.

Mch 14th Our boat steamed over to the Arkansas shore, and we all land for exercise, while the boat is undergoing a thorough cleaning. One of the men

[7]This movement was meant to be a full-scale attack on Fort Pillow, Tennessee; but before the assault began, General Pope's army was ordered to Shiloh.

belonging to another Co. got hold of a can of cherries, sitting under the shade of a tree, he proceded to devour them, seeds and all; some of his comrades wanted a taste, but he got away with the whole lot. But sad to relate, his greed proved his distruction. In two hours he was a dead man; I suppose the cherry stones he swallowed caused his death.

Mch 17th Our whole fleet is ordered to Pittsburg Landing, which is on the Tennessee River. We are soon moving up stream.

19th We have passed New Madrid, and Island #10, Hickman and Columbus Ky. and tie up at Cairo Ill. long enough to take on board all the accumulated mail for the army, also some supplies. Cal and I receive a batch of letters and I receive two boxes by express, one from Will Sutcliffe containing a lot of one and two ounce vials of cholera medicine, a sure shot on stomach troubles. The other box is from Sister Mary, at Providence R.I. and contained some linen shirts for Calvin and myself, just what we need, and they fill a long felt want. The medicine I sell to the boys of our company at 25c and 50c retaining only enough for my own use and Cals. in case of emergency. The fleet again gets under way while Cal and I get off in a corner to enjoy our letters in peace and quiet.

21st We have passed up the Ohio, and into the Tennessee river at Paduca, landing at Shiloh. A great battle has been fought here with our side the victors after a hot struggle.

Traffic to and from Shiloh

At first our army was beaten, by the enemy under Genl [Albert Sidney Johnston] Johnson, later they were victorious.

Our corps arrives too late to participate.

Mch 23d It has been raining with great regularity, mud is the predominant feature of the landscape. Never the less we are tramping along towards Corinth Miss. The road is just horrible, mud puddles, and mud without puddles, we soon leave the wagon train far behind; dividing our lines, we march on either side of the road among the dripping trees, they, the trees are all weeping copiously at the dismal prospect, and their over flowing moisture drenches us, but its better than tramping in the mud. Late in the afternoon we halt near Farmington, and pitch our tents in the woods. The rain is still coming down with increased volume. The mail wagon is here; a letter from Providence for me from sister Mary. It contains the saddest news, that of the death of our dear Mother; after reading it through, I silently pass it to Calvin, and go off into the woods, to brood over the sad news. I think over the past, when we were all at home together, before the war came on, and separated us; then I was careless, like many another boy. How I wished that the old times were with us again, we would show her how her boys would appreciate such a good Mother; vain regrets now, it is to late. The letter said she was in no pain when passing away, but how she must have longed to see her boys who were so far away. We may not see her last resting place until this war is over, if by chance we are spared until then.

I lay down in our tent, and the monotonous sound of the down poor of the rain on its slanting sides, together with my tired condition after the weary days march, I fell asleep. About two o'clock, I woke up with a curious sensation which I did not fully comprehend, until by the aid of a consumtive looking candle stuck in the end of a bayonet, I saw the other boys sitting upon their knap sacks. I realized I was laying in about three inches of water, which the heavy down poor of rain had deluged the grassy floor of our tent. I do not know how long I slept laying in the water, it being a warm night and the water being warm also, together with the fact I was dead tired when I lay down must have kept me oblivious of the flood for some time. However I set up with the rest, for the balance of the night. I was pretty well used to wet clothes both waking and sleeping, so that was of little or no consequence. The elements continued their mighty revelry. The sharp crack of the thunder sounded like the discharge of artillery, while the almost constant play of lightning looked like the flashes of a thousands guns.

Mch 27th Our position is near Farmington which is occupied by the enemys out posts from Corinth Miss. some four or five miles away. The swampy

Corduroy Road—All Hand-labor

nature of the land, makes it impassable for artillery, so the engineer corps have cut a path through the timber, using the trees to make a corduroy road, which will enable us to advance. This morning a force of rebel infantry and artillery came from Corinth, to feel of our position; we were ordered out to meet them, a stiff skirmish took place, with some loss on both sides in wounded. A battalion of our cavalry charged the enemy, and many saddles were emptied, but the rebs. retreated and while the artillery engaged in a duel with the enemys batteries, we were ordered back to camp, about dusk.

Mch 28th Owing to the fact that the roads between here and our base of supplies at the river [are almost impassable] our supply wagons are greatly delayed, and our rations have given out, we have had nothing to eat all day, and we are feeling the pangs of semi starvation. The Hospital department having several barrels of whiskey on hand, a lot of quinine is dumped into it and a gill issued to each man. As a sanitary measure no doubt its a good thing, but as a substitute for food, its a failure. After night had fallen, some wagons came up, and we got a supply of hard tack, bacon and coffee, with which the inner man was soon supplied, to our great satisfaction.

May 9th The sappers and miners have been busy as bees for the last ten days making roads through the swamp. In order that several divisions may ad-

vance in concert, our division march to Farmington[8],
and when through the swamp on to higher ground.
A strong skirmish line is thrown forward, several
batteries and a regiment of cavalry is on our right.
Our skirmish line soon ran against the enemys position; finding them in force, our batteries getting
into commanding positions, open up with rapid firing, which is returned with interest by the rebel batteries. Their shells passing just over us, we are soon
ordered to lay down in line of battle, which the
skirmishers have already done. The rifle balls cut
the air all around us, with a zip! zip! sound, that
makes ones flesh creep. Our cavalry made a gallant
charge, which the enemy repulsed, and many rider-
less horses returned. These maneuvers only intended
as a demonstration, and with no intention of bringing
on a general engagement, we were ordered back, to
camp. Our regiment only met with a slight loss, only
two wounded. The second Lieutenant of our Co.
was sun struck, and was brought in unconscious,
and sent to the hospital.

May 15th Marched around to the right of Corinth,
driving in the rebel out posts, and find the town
strongly fortified, with batteries posted at short intervals within their works. Returned to our camp
after night fall.

[8] By far the best book which covers the campaigns in which
Smith will be engaged from now on is Stanley F. Horn's *The
Army of Tennessee* (Norman, Oklahoma: University of Okla-
homa Press, 1955).

May 18th Late last night our division march out beyond Farmington, form a line, and procede to fortify the position. Our regiments line ran through a grave yard; we did not like the ghastly idea of digging among the graves, but an invading army has no respect for the rights of property or person, alive or dead. The ditch however was dug broader than usual, and shallow enough to not disturb the denisons of the silent city, and by day light, our breastworks were about finished, and the batteries placed in position.

May 20th One of our regimental mules, took it into his long eared pate to get a bad case of glanders, and in order to prevent the disease from spreading to his mulish comrades, Col Bradley ordered our ordinance sergeant Extrand to drive him to the rear and shoot him. Extrand invited me to go along and take a shot at his mule-ship, if a second shot was found necessary. I assisted in driving the animal to a proper distance to the rear of camp. Taking a stand some fifty yards distant, Extrand fired at the mules head but missed his aim, causing the mule to shake his head and look at us. Reloading his enfield, I took careful aim just below the butt of the animals ear and fired, and his muleship droped with a ball through his brain. I was just congratulating myself on the good shot I had made, when a mounted orderly rode up and arrested me for firing a gun in the rear of camp, against postive orders to the contrary from headquarters, said orders of which

I knew nothing about. Being found with the gun in my hands, caught red handed, as it were, I had no choice but to accompany my captor to Genl Popes Quarters; finding him engaged with several officers in consultation, he ordered me to be taken to the provoguards, and to be tied to a tree until he had time to investigate the matter. I had already explained to the guard, that Col. Bradley was the responsible party and as Extrand had returned to camp I supposed my detention would last only a short time. It was about eleven A.M. when we reached the tree, and I was tied to its massive trunk in the loosest manner by my sympathiseing guard, who had no sooner turned his back than I slipped the rope, and lay down in the shade of the friendly tree. The day being warm I soon fell asleep. About noon, the same orderly came and woke me up, having brought me my dinner, which consisted of a plate of chicken soup, some hard tack and stewd chicken. To say I enjoyed this sumptuous repast would be drawing it mildly, and I told my guard if he would arrest me again I would not object, if he would continue to feast me in like manner. He remarked that chickens did not grow on every bush, in fact was a scarce article. Later on I was relieved. Our Quarter Master Capt [Henry] Howland, was sent by Col Bradley to explain matters to the Genl. Returning to Camp, I told the boys, about my dinner, and it made their mouths water, and wish for a like experience.

May 28th With three days rations in our haver sacks, a canteen full of water, sixty rounds of ammunition, our knapsacks on our backs, we break camp, and advance forcing the rebel picket line back into their works. We take up a position by fours, front, ready to wheel into line of battle in a moment.

A battery of six guns, drove up just to our right, was unlimbered and planted, then double shotted, while the caisons were driven off over rising ground and out of sight, and the gunners lay down with their lanyards in hand, and awaited the expected charge of the enemy. Nor had we long to wait, for soon the woods was filled with their yells as they came, with the evident intention of capturing that Yankee battery which to all appearance was innocent of support, our line being formed just behind the timber. On they came in swift advance, yelling like bedlamites let loose; when they had reached a proper distance, up rose the gunners, and fired death and distruction into their ranks. At point blank range wide swaths were cut through the rebel ranks; they staggered and stoped. Another discharge followed and the enemy turned and ran for dear life, back to their works, while shot and shell followed them, leaving their dead and wounded upon the field. We threw up a line of breastworks where we stood, thus gaining a position much nearer to Corinth.

May 29th All day long have the enemy been pounding our works with their artillery but as we lay close behind our works, no one was hit as far as I can learn. When darkness settles over the scene their firing ceases, and we suspect they are preparing to vacate their works.

May 30th At day light our pickets move up cautiously, and discover the empty works; the enemy having evacuated them during the night, our troops advance and occupy the town. A force is started on their track which follow as far as Boonville [Booneville] Miss. capturing numbers of stragglers.

June 3d Returning to Corinth and go into camp out east of town.

July 2d We have remained inactive for the past month, except drilling once each day, living on full rations. A force marched to Danville one day, but found no enemy.

July 4th Spent the day in looking over my correspondence, and writing letters.

July 20th New arms were issued to our regiment today; they are called the Austrian rifles[9], are brand new.

July 21st Break camp, and march eastward along the Memphis and Charleston R R.

July 22nd Pass through Burnshill [Burnsville] and Iuka springs, reaching Tuscumbia Alabama, and go into camp. Here is one of the largest springs I ever saw; the water comes from the base of a small

[9]There were a variety of Austrian rifles imported during the Civil War in a variety of calibers but they were all of one basic design and were all rifle muskets.

mountain, forming a pool deep and wide enough to float a small ship; quite a deep and broad stream is formed from the great volume of water.

July 25th Strike tents at midnight and continue our eastward march, reaching Courtland on the 26th. Here Co's H and K are detached and left behind to guard the R R. About three miles further on Co's E and G go into camp, while our Co. drop out at Trinity station, and the other co's continue on to Decatur. A strong stockade is erected, our tents pitched within the enclosure, loopholes are cut between the standing logs, and we settle down for a rest.

Aug 10th Corp [Benjamin F.] James with nine men started out on a scout, Marching into a deep cut on the R.R. They were ambuscaded, and captured, by a force of rebels.

Aug 12th While one of the men was cleaning his gun it was accidently discharged, the ball passed through the wall of his tent and into the next one severely wounding one of our men. It being purely an accident, although a piece of carelessness, nothing was done.

Aug 24th Two co's of the 27th Ill came up and relieved us, and we marched to Decatur, and found the rest of the regiment, going into camp in the suburbs of the town.

Aug 30th Co's C. G. H and K, went on an expedition into the mountains. Arrived at, and surrounded a house, supposed to contain a squad of rebels. I was placed on post with the picket line, and we watched until the dawn of day. A party of horseman rode up, and being challanged opened fire upon us which we returned, when they fled. We picked up a double barrel shot gun and two hats; we could not tell if any of our shots took effect, as it was not light enough to see. They were the people we came for, but evidently they had been on an expedition of their own, and so were out side our lines, and escaped.

Sept 25th It is reported that the Rebel Genl [Braxton] Bragg is in Ky. with a large force, threatening Nashville, Tenn.

Sept 27th At daylight we are up, get a hasty breakfast, strike tents and heap them up in piles, set them on fire; orders came to make a forced march to Nashville, which is about 200 miles distant. Everything is destroyed that will impede our march, nothing is left to fall into the hands of the rebels. We cross the Tenn. River on a pontoon bridge formed of canvas covered boats; when the whole force is over the pontoons are burnt also, and then we strike out for our destination.

Chapter III

Wherein Smith and his Illinois regiment move straight north from Athens, Alabama, to Columbia, Tennessee, and Smith becomes a member of a hastily formed irregular company of mounted infantry called "Powell's Scouts." The march continues north to Nashville, where Smith chivalrously recovers a colt he had sold to a blind man and his blue-eyed daughter (the colt had been stolen from them by a rascal named Sweeney). "Powell's Scouts" patrol the countryside around Nashville, occasionally meeting and skirmishing with small Confederate units. He visits the Hermitage and continues scouting the roads around Nashville, several times running into Confederates at Stewart's Ferry on Stone's River. As Smith continues on this duty, Bragg's invasion into Kentucky is thwarted and he moves south to Murfreesboro, Tennessee, taking up a position northwest of the city along Stone's River. General William S. Rosecrans (who replaced Buell) moves after careful preparation on Bragg's position, bringing on the Battle of Murfreesboro (or Stone's River) December 31, 1862-January 2, 1863. The Union suffers a defeat, although it does capture Murfreesboro and forces Bragg to retreat to the south. The 51st Illinois is in the battle but

Smith is not, for "Powell's Scouts" continue patrol-
ling near Nashville, once encountering some of
John Hunt Morgan's Confederate cavalry at Stew-
art's Ferry. After continued scouting duty, Smith
escorts Confederate sympathizers out of Union lines
and then escorts a convicted bounty jumper to his
place of execution.

Oct 6th This is the first opportunity I have found
to write up my journal of events, since leaving Decatur, and bidding good by to old Alabama. We
have made rapid progress, have passed through
Athens Ala, Elkton and Pulaski Tenn, and are now
at Columbia, in camp on Duck River. Our rear
guards and column en-march have been harassed
continually by mounted guerillas and bushwhackers,
who would ride within range, fire at us and ride
away, repeating the operation further on. There is
only a small squad of cavalry with us, some dozen or
so, belonging to the 7th Ill Cav, and are used as an
advance guard, so we have been at the mercy of the
rebels.

Two days ago, our Genl, growing very tired of
this one sided business, gave orders, that if any of
our men should happen to find a horse to mount
him. Heretofore strict orders were given, that no
one should leave the ranks but when the latter orders came notwithstanding the fact that the country
seemed to be entirely unpeopled with any sort of

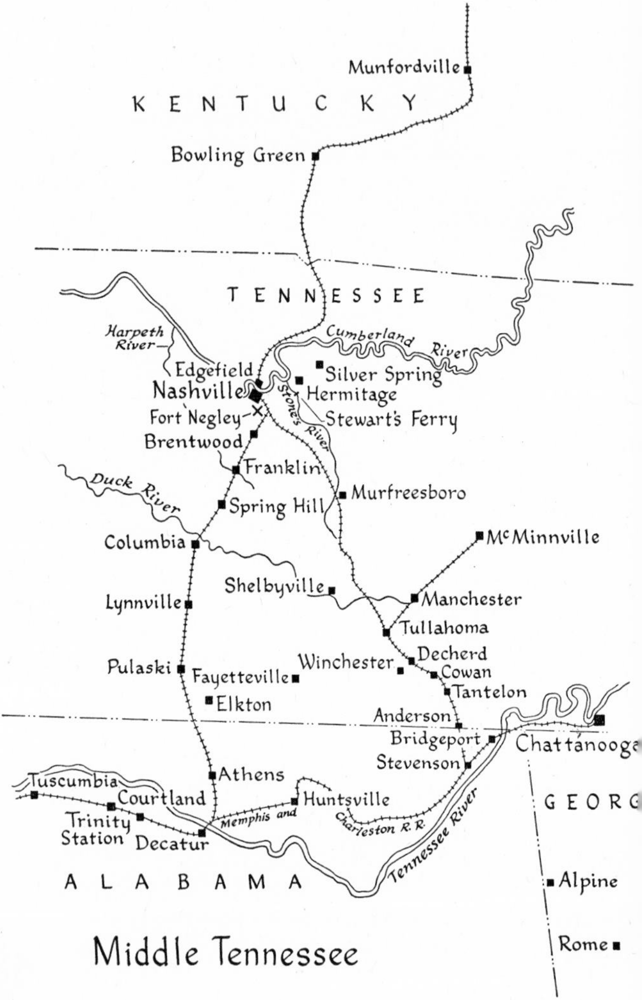

Middle Tennessee

four footed animals, how fast the said quadrupeds materialized. The day had only half gone, when a hundred had been discovered, each one was mounted by a soldier astride his back. In fact saddles and bridles were much scarcer than animals, for only about half the number had them. I secured a fine black mare, without even leaving the ranks. As our co was passing a plantation, an old darky rode out of the gate with the intention of following the yankeys to freedom. He was leading another animal upon which was perched his little boy. There was a chance which I grasped in a moment. I said to the darkey, here you Sambo can't you ride double. Take your boy up behind you, All right Massa. All right sar, while I put the boy behind him and putting my blanket upon the mare's back, was mounted in a jiffy. So I became one of the famous one-hundred. About half of us were sent to the rear as a guard, while the rest covered the flanks, and when the bush-whackers opened fire after that we gave chase as best we could, but carrying a long rifle while riding at full speed, was no Joke. While we could not come up with the rebs, we sent some bullets after them, which finally had the desired effect, of causing them to quit fooling around in our vicinity. But we were truly an awkward squad. Some of the boys, were mounted on mules, and they as well as many of the horses objected to our firing over their heads, and while they kicked and thrashed around, a few of the riders were dumped in the road, but fortunately no body was hurt, but it was a wonder we did not shoot each other, accidently of course, though no such unlucky thing took place.

Oct 10th Continuing our march, pass through Franklin and Brentwood reach the outskirts of Nashville, and go into camp, Our mounted co. still together.

Oct 15th Our troops marched into town, and being supplied with tents, formed a camp. Those of us who were mounted, rode down to the foot of Cherry street, with Capt [Frank] Powell in charge, and took possession of an old deserted powder mill. While the 19th Ill was on their way, and passing a house, some one fired a shot at them from an upper window. A Co. surrounded the house, and in searching it, found a man and woman, whom they arrested, then burned the house down.

Oct 16th Our Company was disbanded, sixty five of our number remained (I was one of the lucky ones), and reorganized into a company of mounted scouts, and were regularly detailed by order of Genl [John M.] Palmer, Capt Powell[1] in command, with Lieut Grow 1st Lieut. Sergeants and Corporals were elected by the Co, orderly Sergt Parks, Wyman 2d Sergt, while I was elected 8th Corporal;

[1] The commander of this impromptu and irregular group of mounted men was Frank Powell, who enlisted as the First Sergeant of Company H, 7th Michigan Infantry. He was discharged on Nov. 11, 1861 and reentered service a week later as Captain of Company I, 14th Michigan Infantry. He was discharged February 25, 1865.

we procured some gold braid and sewed it upon our sleeves according to rank.

Oct 17th I purchased a young horse of a citizen, who recommended the animal for speed. Well he proved to be speedy enough, but proved to be too young to stand much hardship, so Luke (my bunk mate) and I rode up town leading the colt and without much trouble found a purchaser. The man was blind, so he judged the animal by the sence of touch, feeling him pretty much all over. He also used his eighteen year old daughter's judgment—whose eyes were not blind, but they were a handsome pair, (the eyes I mean), blue as the sky. I disposed of the colt to them, he paying me part down and later in the day I was to call for the balance.

So late in the afternoon Luke and I rode over to the place, and found the poor old blind fellow in a terrible way, while the pretty daughter was drownded in tears. I enquired as to their troubles and learned that shortly before we arrived, a citizen, one S.S. Sweeney they said, claimed the colt, they asked him to wait until I came, but that was not his ticket, so in spite of their protests he led the colt off. I got a discription of the gent, together with the fact they knew him to be a tough character. I told the old fellow I would try and find the thief, and bring the horse back if possible, so we rode over to Cherry St, not knowing which way to go. Turning down towards camp, about the first man we met was the one I was looking for; he was riding the colt and leading

another horse. He was a big burly fellow, with his
bad character written all over him; we halted him,
and I told him to get off that horse instanter. I
could see he knew what I meant, but he was, or pre-
tended to be half full, and commenced to tell a
rambling story about how he bought the animal of a
soldier, which I cut short by pulling my revolver on
him, and gave him ten seconds to give up the horse.
He looked down the barrel of my gun an instant,
and the way he slid off that horse made Luke laugh,
and it was comical, but I was'nt in any humor to
laugh just then. In less time than it takes to tell
about it, he transferred his saddle to the other horse
and gave Luke the end of the halter. Still covering
him, I told him to git, which he made haste to do,
but turned round when at some distance and shook
his fist at me, with curses on his lips and vengance

Cavalry on Patrol

in his eye. I led the colt back to his owner who received him with many thanks, and I received the balance of the money from the pretty daughter, also her grateful thanks, which was gracefully given and so my first horse trading was done.

Oct 18th We receive orders to turn over all our long guns, and such horses as are not suitable to our work. Suitable horses are issued to us, and full trappings, such as the regular Cavalry use, also the Burnsides breech loading carbines[2], a nine inch navy revolver[3], and cavalry saber. Being now thoroughly organized, all through the orders of Genl Jno M Palmer, we are named the Powells Scouts. The company is composed mainly of young men, with myself the youngest of the lot, with a few gray heads. Two of our members are quarter breed Indians, Bill Chatfield and Bill Westbrook from Michigan.

Oct 25th Sergeant Parks having posted himself in cavalry tactics, is drilling the Co. daily, which we all take to with much interest, and our horses most of them, seem to take kindly to the training, also. My horse is a remarkably intelligent animal, he is about six years old and a swift runner; we go through

[2]The Burnside carbine had been invented by Ambrose E. Burnside before the war. In 1861 it was 7¼ pounds in weight, 54 caliber, with a 21 inch barrel, and was loaded at the breech with either a brass or wrapped foil cartridge.

[3]This was presumably the Colt .36 caliber single action navy revolver, a very popular Civil War hand gun. The 9″ barrel is unusual, the more common lengths were from one to three inches shorter.

the Evolutions, such as riding in all gates, jumping logs and ditches, firing from their backs, over their heads, charging with sabers drawn, standing on the ground and firing over the saddle &c. A few of the horses, learn as easy as a boy his A.B.C's, while others, do not learn nearly so quick.

Oct 26th I am ordered to take one man and ride out on the Murphysboro [Murfreesboro] pike, patrolling for four hours before midnight. I take Bill Chatfield with me. After receiving the countersign from the Captain, I give it to Bill, and we pass through our outer picket line, ride a few miles beyond them; without encountering any thing of a suspicious nature, we return within the lines about midnight, spread our blankets under a tree, and turn in, sleep until day break. We find an inch of snow covering our rubber blankets, but I was oblivious of any cold. Saddled our horses, and took a run of about two miles out and back, and returned to camp and breakfast.

Oct 29th A party of mounted rebels, made a dash at our picket line, and firing a volley, rode away. Word was brought to Capt Powell, he hastily mounted nineteen of us, and we rode with all speed to the scene of action. Lear[n]ing the direction the rebs had gone, we started at top speed, about a mile out we ran on to them, taking them by surprise, most of them were dismounted and we fired into them while going at a galop; about twenty were in sight, and they returned our fire and fled, all except three whom we cut off from their horses, and captured. No one was hit except Billy [Marion] Maron, who caught a glancing bullet on his scabbard which left a dent in the steel. We took our prisoners into town and turned them over to the guards at Genl. Palmers HeadQuarters.

Oct 30th Genl P, rode down to our camp accompanied by a company of the 7th Ill. Cav., gave order to the Capt. to mount the full company and go as advance guard on a reconnoitering expedition. About five miles out on the Murphysboro pike, we discovered a nest of rebels. The Capt ordered us to deploy as skirmishers; getting close on to the enemy, we drop in a volley, which is returned, without effect as we were in skirmishing line, with a wide space between each four men. The 7th came up with a rush, and we all charged with a yell. The rebs seeing our reinforcements waited not upon the order of their going but went at once. They left one killed, and six prisoners fell into our hands, which we took into town. The most of these rebs we run across are roving bands, of tough cases banded together, for mutual strength; while they are Confederates, they belong to no part of the rebel army, and rob friend and foe alike. In breaking up these squads of freebooters, for our own safety, we incidently are protecting the families of confederate soldiers, whom these guerillas rob.

Nov 5th This morning a large force of the enemy, made a demonstration all along our front. They placed a battery on an elevation near the Chicken

Pike and shelled the town and Fort Neglie [Negley];
Our camp being near the Fort, many of the shells
falling short, droped into our camp and exploded.
The Capt. had the bugler sound the call to saddle,
and we mounted, riding out of range. It was soon
discovered that the intention of the rebels, was merely
to keep our attention, while the Rebel Genl [John
H.] Morgan was making a raid over the Cumberland
River in Edgefield, with a view to burning the R R
Bridge which spanned it. But the raid was not a success, owing to the stubborn resistance of the 10th Ill
which held a position on the Gallatin Pike; Morgan
finding his forces repulsed, gave it up for a bad job,
and retreated. About 4. P.M. our Co. rode out on the
Chicken Pike, but we discovered no enemy.

Nov 7th A squad of our Co. scouted the Granny
White pike, discovered a rebel officer and one private, attempting to go southward we ran them down,
and captured them after a hard chase.

Nov 12th We have had no mail from the North for
some time; Genl Bragg holds the R R in Ky, tearing up miles of rails and burning bridges. Today the
mail came by boat; I received ten letters, which I
proceed to inspect with great interest.

Nov 13th A Brigade of infantry ordered to march
out on the Lebanon pike to stone bridge, our Co. go
as advance guard. Reaching the bridge we learn that
nineteen of the 4th Mich Cavalry were surprised
and captured here by a force of rebel Cavalry. The
brigade go into camp, and we return to town.

Nov 14th Under charge of Lieut. Grow twenty five of our Co. go out scouting, as far as the Hermatige [Hermitage]. This is the former home and present burial place of Genl Andrew Jackson who was president in 1832. The present owner is an adopted son, who is said to be a violent secessionist. The place must have been a fine one in its palmy days, but now through neglect its pretty well run to weeds. The drive way is flanked on either side by stately elms, with their overarching bows intermingling. This leads up to the front of the fine old brick mansion. An old decript negress here spends her declining days, basking in the rays of the sun, nursing her crooked fingers, and bent and aged limbs and rheumatic joints. I asked her some questions, as to age, and if she knew the Genl in life. De Lord bless you massa, she replied, I don holl him in dese here arms, when he were only so high, streatching forth her withered hand knee high. Bressed Old Massa, I done nurse him many times, and she turned her toothless visage up to the sun. I all most believed her as her wrinkled face bore the stamp of great age, and if she had said she was the mother of Matheusiler [Methuselah], I was not prepared to contradict her. The tomb of Jackson is situated in one corner of the garden, and is quite well preserved, stone pillars, supporting a canopied roof, the floor cemented, under which the remains are deposited. After inspecting every thing of interest we return to Camp, our visit recalled to mind, how Jackson

fought at New Orleans, the british in the war of
1812 to 15, and how in 32, when South Carolina attempted to secede from the union, as it did do last
year, and how he sent a war vessel into Charleston
Harbor, and threatened to blow the city out of exis-
tance if they persisted. This time we had not a Jackson as president, but a Beauchanen [Buchanan],
and there's the diference.

Nov 16th Full co escort two wagon loads of mail
for Genl Crittendons [Thomas L. Crittenden] camp
at Silver Springs.

Nov 18th I am ordered to take charge of a squad
of the Co. and scout one of the pikes, decided to try
the Granny White pike, we ran across two rebels,
home on leave from their army. After a short hot
chase, we capture both. While returning to town,
discover a small drove of turkeys; while these birds
do not hold quite as an exalted a position as our
american eagle, yet we know they make much finer
eating, and so we gather in a few of them. Turn
over our prisoners to Hdqrs. the two without feath-
ers, but the turkeys are destined to feed the hungry
scouts.

Nov 23d I am promoted from 8th to 3d Corporal,
and carry some important dispatches from Genl
[James D.] Morgan to Genl Palmer.

25th Orderly Sergt Parks is ordered out with
twenty of the Co in a beef foraging expedition; we
capture a small drove, for which vouchers are given
on Unkle Sam.

27th I go on a scout accompanied by Luke and Marion. About noon, we came to a promising look-ing house, and on motion of Luke, seconded by Marion, and unanimously carried, that we apply for dinner. Leaving Marion on guard without the gate, where he could get a good view of the road in both directions Luke and I make an advance upon the citadel; we found the head of the house a widow, or so she claims to be, although I imagine her better half is in the rebel Army. She has a daughter who is about 18 and who frankly states she has a sweet heart in the rebel army. Stating our mission to be in search of the wherewithal to replenish the inner man, the lady invites us in and gets up a dinner for us in good shape, then Luke relieves Marion while he comes in for his share, after which I liquidate with a ten dollar confederate bill, which is about the figure in that kind of money, and with which we are generally well supplied. Return to town without having seen any thing that looked like a Jonny reb.

Nov 29th Sergt Parks with about twenty five of us out on a scout. We soon left the pike and, rode in a south westerly direction into a thickly wooded part of the country, which was new to us. After rid-ing many miles, following a cowpath, which nar-rowed to such an extent that we were compelled to go in single file, like Indians on a lost trail. Keeping on, we discovered a small clearing in the midst of thick surrounding timber. In the center of the clearing was a log house, delapidated in appearance.

On our approach there issued from the hingeless doorway, an old gray headed man whose long hair and longer gray beard gave him the appearance of a much self neglected mortal; following upon his heels there came six women of various ages ranging from twenty to fifty. While we drew up in line watching the procession, a stream of shock headed, and barefooted children filed out into view, numbering nearly a score. I wondered if we had not discovered an isolated old morman who had fallen out of the ranks and came here in these wilds, and started a colony of his own. Judging from their concentrated gaze which they leveled upon us in a body, they must have been greatly interested in the first lot of genuine Yankees they had ever beheld. The old fellow must have had a private still of his own, for after he had sized us up, he brought out a mammoth jug of moon shine whiskey, and a gourd, which he offered to us. Many of the Co partook of the beverage, and said it was the genuine stuff; about forty dollars of confederate money was tendered and accepted for the treat.

On the enquiry of Sergt Parks as to whether any rebs came around that section, the old fellow replied in the negative, and certainly from the general appearance of poverty which pervaded the surroundings, no one would ever return for booty a second time; and how in the world he managed to feed so many mouths was a mystery, one we did not care to investigate so we left them and returned to town.

Nov 30th Capt. Powell headed a squad of twenty two of us, riding out on the chicken pike, one of our almost daily scouts. Crossing the ford at Stewarts ferry rode up the hill by fours front with Corp. Lakey and three men a few yards in advance. They gained the brow of the hill, when, bang! bang! they received a volley. Capt Powell ordered us into line, we put the spurs to our horses, and dashed up the hill at full speed, getting into two lines, at once, on rising the brow of the hill, we discovered a squad of the enemy charging us up their side of the hill. Yelling like fiends, and firing at us, a volley was sent at them, and we loaded up again, they checked up, and a second volley followed and drawing our six shooters, the capt ordered a charge at the top of his lungs. The rebs fled for all they were worth, and we after them, down hill over the roughest road we ever traveled at a break neck speed. In fact it was as rough as the celebrated road to Jordon, but at the risk of breaking some of our necks, we pushed after our game. They were mounted on the best horse flesh the country afforded, and so they out ran us, and we returned to the scene of action. Lakeys horse being stiff in the fore shoulders could not be turned quick enough to suit him, so he slid off his back and made a dive over a fence into a field. As the rebs were charging the other three joined us as we rode up, we found a loose rebel horse with all his equipments, but his rider had disappeared among the thick cedars that lined one side of the road, whether wounded or not we did not know. The captured horse we took with us; on riding back to the ferry, stoped at a citizens house, who told the Capt, the rebs was some of Dick McCann's[4] men, and there was twenty eight of them, mostly armed with double barreled shot guns. Dick is the leader of about fifty of the most notorious guerrillas and freebooters. Rode back to camp. After supper I took eleven men and rode back to Stewarts ferry to watch the ford all night. I placed two men on each side of the road leading down to the river, retiring about a hundred yards in reserve, posting a relief about every two hours, taking my turn with the men. Nothing of a suspicious nature occurred during the night, and at dawn we retired to camp.

Dec 1st The whole Company receive orders to go out to Stone bridge and camp, so as to be near to, and guard Stewarts Ferry.

[4] Richard McCann was Major of the 9th Tennessee Cavalry, active in the Murfreesboro-Chattanooga-McMinnville area from the fall of 1862 until captured on August 19, 1863. He was considered by most Union soldiers to be a notorious guerrilla raider. McCann was not released from a Union prisoner of war camp until January 20, 1865. The official report of this affair is as follows:

"A scouting party of 25 mounted infantry, under the command of Captain Powell, was sent out on the Statesville road yesterday. They met a party of guerrillas about 7 miles out, drove in their advance, taking 2 rifles and 1 horse. The main body was found strongly posted on the opposite side of a creek, and in number three or four to one. The captain thought it advisable not to attack them, his command being poorly armed."

O.R., I, 20, pt. 1, p. 27.

Dec 3d Corp. Coppage and I with sixteen men are detailed to videt the ford for twenty four hours, trouble being expected from that quarter. On the morning of the 4th nine men come out and relieve us. During the night we were aroused by hearing shots in the direction of the ferry. The Co. saddled up at once, and galloped out to the ferry. Meeting the reserve. it is learned, that they had been fired into while laying around a fire. The rebs had come up in the darkness, and attacked without warning[5]; the corporal had made the mistake of not posting a man to guard the reserve, as well as the ferry. The rebs escaped in the darkness of the timber. We found one man wounded with two buck shot, (Smith) and poor Gorman was riddled with seven. Gorman died

[5]The official report of that affair by Brigadier James D. Morgan reads:

"This morning about 3 o'clock a sergeant and 9 men of Captain Powell's company mounted scouts, stationed at Stewart's Ford, 2½ miles on our right, were attacked by a mounted force of the enemy of about 60 men. All of our men succeeded in making their escape, with their arms and accouterments, but with the loss of their horses. Two were wounded, 1 severely. The enemy made their approach upon our right from the direction of the Murfreesborough pike. I have no cavalry to cover my flank in that direction. I had supposed that vedettes were stationed from the Murfreesborough pike toward my right.

I sent out yesterday a foraging party about 4 miles to the front, on the Lebanon pike; 2 men were taken, 1 a mounted scout of Captain Powell's Company, and a teamster; they were paroled and returned to camp almost as soon as the train. I returned them to duty, ignoring the paroles, and with orders that they be charged with the arms lost."
O.R., I, 20, pt. 1, p. 30.

at day light and his body we conveyed to town; Smith's wounds were slight, one horse was killed, and five were wounded. The buck shot indicated that the rebs were armed with shot guns. Perhaps they were some of McCann's men bent on revenge.

Dec 8th Genl Jas Morgan came out to inspect Stewards ferry, and we were ordered to return to town as advance to a brigade of infantry that had come out. Reaching our old camp, tents were struck, and we pitched them on a vacant piece of ground at the corner of summer and oak Sts. Raised bunks are constructed, and a long shed on the premises is utilized for our horses.

Dec 10th A rumor has reached us that we will disband and return to our respective commands. We are considerably put out at this, until later orders came from Genl [William S.] Rosecrans, that in as much as our services during our organization had proved very satisfactory, we will continue the same, as scouts, videts, escorts &c as heretofore, and placed under the immediate command of Genl Jas Morgan. All the old horses are exchanged for better ones, and, "Richard is himself again."

Dec 31st Have, in the past ten days, made several scouts, acted as videts, escort &c; we captured two prisoners near stone bridge, who were at Murphysboro, and we learn that a great battle is going on at Stone River, some twenty miles south. The old 51st is out there, and Calvin with Co "C". I shall look anxiously for more news, until I learn he is safe.

Jany 1st 1863 Another year has passed away and the war seems as far from ending as a year ago. The old year was ushered out and the new year comes in, while the great battle goes on. Curriers are coming in with news of the strife; the Division occupying the right of our army, was fiercely attacked by the enemy, and becoming some what demoralized, retreated. Genl. Rosecrans Commanding all of our forces, personally rallied our men, and by a vigorous attack drove the enemy back and saved the day; and there is one more victory marked upon our banners.

Jany 5th I heard from Cal today, and he is all right. Co. "C" lost some killed and wounded. A portion of the Co. captured a lot of prisoners.

12th Our Co is ordered out on the Franklin Pike; we met a young lady in a buggy, who gave Capt Powell some secret information which must have been of considerable importance, as we rode back to town at once, and the Capt reported to Genl Morgan.

15 & 16th A blizzard is upon us accompanied by a heavy fall of snow. We stick close to our camp fires, while it lasts.

23d Our tent mess consists of Corps Culkin and myself, and privates Morse, Luke and Marion. We went out on a scout today, and surprised three rebels, who surrendered on demand, and we took them to Gen Morgan.

Jany 30th Capt Powell headed twenty four of us, and we rode to Stewarts Ferry. On arriving in its vicinity, Sergt Wyman took charge, while the Capt took five men, and rode down around the bluff which faces the ferry. They had passed from our sight hardly three minutes, when several shots were fired. We rode forward to investigate, and formed line on the brow of the bluff over looking the ferry. We discovered the flat boat which is used to cross the ferry just about to land on the opposite bank with some thirty or more men, and upon the bank was some fifty or more mostly mounted, but they were all dressed in blue uniform. Capt Powell and four of our men were on the boat just landing. For one instant we thought these troops belonged to our army, as they wore Unkle Sams blue, but the next moment we knew they were Confederates, and were about to open fire on them, when Sergt Wyman said no. You might hit the capt. or our own men. Why they did not open fire upon us at once seemed strange as we sat upon our horses in plain view of the rebs. All this took place within a moment or two, while hesitating undecided what course to pursue, we saw about half of them gallop off down the opposite bank of the river on the main pike at stone bridge, with a view to cut off our retreat to town. Then we started back in the same direction, and met Bill Westbrook who had accompanied the capt. he was riding his horse as stiff as a ram rod, with his hand pressed tightly upon his right breast, where he was shot clear through his lungs and body. Two of us rode on each side to keep him on his horse and resumed our retreat. At the first house, we left Bill, in charge of the people who promised to put him to bed at once, and take care of him until we sent out a surgeon from town.

Then we rode for all the horses could go, and reached the main pike, seeing nothing more of the rebs, whom we knew had some distance further to ride on their side of the river. After riding a mile or so, we slowed down to a more leisurely gate, so if the rebs continued to follow us, we might get them to chase us near enough to our picket line to get them into trouble, but evidently they had given up the chase. So we reported the affair to Genl Morgan, and then sent an ambulence and surgeon out to poor Bill. Westbrook is a quarter breed indian with a constitution like a bronco so we did not give him up altogether.

31st He was brought in this evening and placed in the hospital. In comparing notes about the days adventure, several of us noticed a singular thing while inspecting the rebels. It was noticed that a great many of their horses had two nose bags attached to either their saddles or straped on their necks, all of which seemed to be full of something. An unusual thing for mounted men to carry more than one, if any at all. Here was a mystery; they must have been bent upon some raid of importance, and their meeting with us may have caused them to post pone it.

Jany 31st Capt Powell being a prisoner Lieut Grow takes command of our Co. I visit the Hospital,

and find Westbrook as comfortable as his condition
will admit. He said it did not hurt him much to
talk. The Dr. when he got to him at the citizens
house, proceeded to dress his wound, and the first
operation was probing a silk handkerchief clear
through his body, following the straight course the
ball had made. He informed me, that when the Capt
and four men started for the ferry, he followed
them. Coming in sight of the river, they saw some
twenty men just landing, and they being in blue
uniform, supposed they belonged to our army, but
took the precaution to challenge them; they answered they belonged to the 5th Tenn. Cavalry.
This being a union regiment, all suspicion, If the
Capt had any was dismissed, and they rode up to
them, when they were immediately surrounded by
the enemy with drawn revolvers. As soon as Bill
took in the situation, as quick as a flash he wheeled
his horse, and dashed up the hilly road; a dozen
shots followed him, only one hit him, which he
said nearly knocked him off his horse. He said he
held on by his knees and the horses neck. Brave old
Bill.

Feb 5th Genl Morgans head quarters, burned to
the ground today. He occupied a private house together with his staff. Fire supposed to have origi-
nated from a defective flue.

March 8th Our force at Franklin were attacked.
It is eighteen miles south of Nashville; the attack
was merely a brush, a sort of feeler by the enemy.

Mch 11th The Co. go out to a place called Slip-up, and continue on towards Stewarts ferry. It is a standing question among us, when we start for that place, as to what we will find. It seems to be a fatal spot for the scouts, nearly all our losses, have occurred there, and whose turn will come next. To day we were agreeably surprised to find it, bathed in sunshine, and peaceful as a summer day, where at some of the boys expressed disappointment, at its deserted appearance.

Mch 25th A detachment of infantry, located at Brentwood, nine miles out on the Franklin Pike. They numbered about four hundred; were attacked by a force of the enemy and after a sharp skirmish, were surrounded and captured. We receive orders to saddle up, and make a run for the place, and in about one hour and a half arrive there only to find the smoldering ruins of the late camp.

April 8th Ordered out as advance for a Division of infantry, and locate with them at Brentwood.

20th Are still located here, at B— we all rode into Nashville to draw our pay, returning again to camp.

21st A part of our Co. take a scout towards Franklin, turning off to the left, we follow a cow path through the woods for several miles, reach a clearing where in is located a fort occupied by a regiment of our troops, returning to camp in time for supper.

At the usual time for retireing I roll my self in my blanket expecting to enjoy a good sleep. At midnight I was called up with orders to carry some dispatches to the fort we had visited during the afternoon. There being no moon, nor stars visible, as it was a cloudy night; it was about as dark as Egypt.

As I rode along the pike, the question very naturally came up as to knowing when to turn off into the woods, however judging the distance as best I could, I trusted the instinct of my horse to find it. Nor was I mistaken in so doing; going along at a swinging gallop, she made a dive into the woods. It was dark enough on the road, but among the timber it was ten fold darker if that were possible, so I gave up the idea of trying to guide the animal and let her have her head. She continued still at a sharp canter winding in and out among the trees, always keeping in the path as I knew by the sound of her hoofs coming in contact with the soft earth; laying low on her neck to avoid over-hanging limbs, the five miles was quickly covered without a mishap. Drawing rein near the clearing, I was challenged by one of the pickets, ordered to dismount and give the countersign; advancing on foot I leaned over the point of the guards bayonet and gave it, and mounting again rode to the fort. Delivering my dispatches to the Commander, I turned into one of the tents, for a rest and sleep; after rubbing my horse down with a wisp of hay, I patted her on the neck for her good behavior, and she rubbed her nose against me as much as to say I am your friend, a fact I well knew, and I was greatly attached to her, as she was always ready and willing to do my bidding. At day break I was up, and gave her a good feed, and breakfasted with the boys, then leisurely rode back to camp.

22d Our Co. is ordered back to our old camp in Nashville.

April 27th We saddle up at midnight and go out on the Granny White pike. After riding for about two hours, we silently surround a house, and await daylight; said house was supposed to contain a squad of rebels who had rendezvous there. At the first dawn of day we close in, and capture the house, but find no enemy. The house was deserted, so we beat a retreat back to town, empty handed.

May 6th For the past few days, we have been engaged in acting as escort to families and persons whose proclivities are all southern; while residing within our lines, they have rendered their sympathy and aid when opportunity offered to the confederates. In consequence of this, the rebel forces have been well informed as to the disposition of our troops and defenses. So by order of the commander, they were given a few days notice each, and then we would escort them beyond our lines and well on their way south[6], and thus we got rid of a danger-

[6]General Orders No. 43, Headquarters Department of the Cumberland, March 8, 1863 ordered southern sympathizers who did not "acknowledge their obligations as citizens of the United States" and who did not give the non-combatants oath and bond would be sent south of Union lines within ten days. General Orders No. 74, April 8, 1863, listed 41 individuals or families by name that were "citizens of Nashville and vicinity" and were to be sent south outside Union lines.

ous element. The majority of them belong to upper tendom, who ride in their own conveyances or mounted.

May 15th We are called upon to perform an unpleasant duty today, no less then to guard a prisoner, from the jail to the place where he was executed. He was a foreigner and had practiced bounty jumping, enlisting as a substitute, for as large a bounty as he could get, he at the first opportunity would desert, make his way north, and repeat the same program. He was tried and convicted. The grave was dug, the box in which he was to be buried, placed near it; seated upon his coffin blind-folded, his hand tied behind his back, twelve soldiers, chosen by lot, from the infantry, drew up in line ten paces distant, six of their guns loaded with ball, and six with blanks. The guns being loaded by others, they none of them knew which had the fatal balls. At the word they took aim and fired. The victim fell back with four bullets in his breast and was buried at once[7].

[7]This was apparently Private Julius Mileka of Company E, 10th Michigan Volunteer Infantry. He deserted from Company E September 14, 1862 and re-enlisted in Company K, 1st Tennessee Infantry on November 6; he seems to have been guilty of a similar pattern of bounty jumping prior to September, 1862. General Orders 100, Headquarters Department of the Cumberland, May 4, 1863, order him shot at noon, May 15, 1863.

CHAPTER IV

Wherein "Powell's Scouts" are disbanded and, on May 29, 1863, Smith is assigned back to Company C, 51st Illinois, at Murfreesboro; three days later he is reassigned to his division headquarters, then commanded by General Philip H. Sheridan, to serve as escort and orderly. Smith moves south with the Army of the Cumberland as Rosecrans in what is called the Tullahoma campaign, begins to manuever Bragg out of Tennessee. Shelbyville and Manchester fall, and Bragg retreats to Chattanooga; Sheridan's division is held near Winchester for a while and then marches southeast to Stevenson, Alabama, on the north side of the Tennessee River. Near here Smith talks with a Confederate picket, visits the large Anderson plantation, moves with his headquarters to Bridgeport, Tennessee, and crosses the river on September 2. Marching over Raccoon Mountain to Trenton, Georgia, thence over Lookout Mountain and turning southwest and away from Chattanooga, Sheridan's Division arrives at Alpine, Georgia, on September 11. Meanwhile Bragg evacuates Chattanooga and concentrates his army behind Chickamauga Creek near Lafayette, Georgia. Rosecrans believing Bragg's evacuation of Chattanooga is a headlong retreat, splits his pursuing army into

*three segments, separated by many miles of moun-
tainous country. The Union Army is thus split so
that General Crittenden is with the 21st Corps to
the north near Chattanooga, General Thomas with
the 14th Corps is in the middle at Stevens Gap near
Trenton, Georgia, and General McCook (whose
20th corps includes Sheridan's division) is farthest
south at Alpine, Georgia. Bragg's plan is to defeat
Rosecrans by attacking his widely separated units
one at a time (Bragg is about to be re-inforced by
Longstreet's units from the east). Rosecrans, now
awake to his danger, hurriedly concentrates his
forces by moving his southern units north to the
Stevens Gap area, extending his center units northward and moving Crittenden from the north down
towards the center. And so the stage is set for the
bloody Battle of Chickamauga.*

May 27th Orders received this morning for our
Company to disband, and each member to report
to the division Head Quarters, in which his regiment is located. Although we were some what prepared for something of this kind, yet it caused considerable regret at the separation about to take
place. A close brotherly feeling had sprang up
among most of us, engendered by our being an independent command, and by the fact that we were
always associated together in our daily scouts, and

duties of every nature pertaining thereto, encountering many dangers. All this tended to cement a lasting friendship among us. All our horses, tents &c also our arms, were turned over to the Quarter Master.

May 29 Transportation being furnished, those of us that belong to Genl [Philip H.] Sheridans division[1], after a general farewell all around, we take the train for Murphysboro. On arriving at HdQrs. and reporting, we are returned to our several Companies. I find old Co "C" in camp and report to Lieut Tilton for duty, am welcomed back by Bro Cal and the rest of the boys, and find myself once more at home in the infantry.

June 1st Lieut Tilton received an order from Capt [George] Lee the AAG to Sheridan, for me to report at HdQrs. at once, for duty. This was a surprise to me, an agreeable one though. Upon reaching there I found Wm Morse had also been detailed, with several others including old Mitchel, all ex members of the scouts. Morse belonged to the 42d Ill.

Each of us receive a horse and equipments, a saber and revolver, and are informed that our duties are to consist, of acting as escort and orderlies to Genl Sheridan.

[1]Major General Philip H. Sheridan's command was the 3rd Division of the 20th Army Corps (Major General Alexander McD. McCook) of Major General William S. Rosecrans' Army of the Cumberland.

21st There is general activity going on in the whole army of the Cumberland, getting ready for a grand campaign, a forward movement is looked for shortly.

June 24th At the first streaks of the coming day, the Army of the Cumberland is roused up, and set to for an early breakfast. After a long period of fine weather, it has changed suddenly and a fine penetrating rain has set in, and this is the appointed day for the opening of the campaign. After the thorough preparation which has been gone through, the mere incident of adverse weather is no consideration. After breakfast, the camp is broken up, and the army is put in motion; Division after Division march out, and take the different roads assigned to them, all verging southward. Our Division marches out on the Shelbyville pike. At about seven miles out, we find a force of the enemy who retreat after a short sharp skirmish. Forward again and go into camp in some timber. A drizzling rain has fallen all day.

25th Still raining, and we are again on the march. The roads are in fearful condition, dry creeks are now swollen streams. Capt Powell of the old scouts, has come up, having been exchanged together with the four men. We learn the particulars of his capture which is as Bill Westbrook told it to me while he was in the hospital; but we learn further that the scout we made on that day, turned out of vast importance to the Goverment, although we were ignorant of its import then. It seems that the force

Cavalry Band with Sheridan

that captured the Capt was a lot of eighty picked men with rebel Genl John Morgan leading them. They were all disguised in blue uniforms, which had been captured from some federal wagon train. At the time spoken of, a large fleet of steam boats had come up the Cumberland river, and were lying at the levee, loaded down with rations, ammunition and clothing, supplies for the army of the Cumberland, for the campaign just started. Genl Morgans plan, was to pass through our picket line after dark ostensively as a body of Union Cavalry from some out laying force, not a very difficult matter in their yankee blue clothes. Once within the lines, they would meet no more pickets, and, riding into town to the levee where the loaded transports lay, separate into squads of a dozen men each, go on board the boats and set fire to them, with cedar shavings and balls of candle wick well saturated with oil, which they carried in their horses nose bags, which we noticed they had with them on that day. All this could have been easily done, and in the confusion which would naturally follow incident to the excitement caused by the burning boats, they could ride back to the picket line and make a dash through it, with not much danger of being shot in the uncertainty of the darkness, a bold exploit certainly, but one worthy of the man who planed it, to be as boldly carried out by a man like Genl John Morgan. But the whole thing fell through, when our Co of scouts met them at Stewarts ferry, as their presence, we would be sure to report, on our return to town, and they had to content themselves with the Capt and four men as prisoners. Thus what would have been, if successfully accomplished; a celebrated raid, a chapter of history added to the war records. It was turned to naught, and the government saved a heavy loss. And perhaps this Campaign would have been delayed, until a new supply fleet could bring us supplies. The Capt said, that while they were held as prisoners, they were well treated. Morgan would allow none of his men to abuse them in any manner; he spoke very highly of his (Morgans) gentlemanly qualities.

26th We are still going southward, and the rain which continues in spasmodict spurts is loath to leave us. Our progress is some what retarded by the bad roads, our long line of wagon trains move very slowly.

27th We made a hard days march, some light skirmishes occurred. The rebels are governing their retreat by our movements.

28th Captured Shelbyville today with a few prisoners.

29th Pass through Manchester Tenn. The enemy reported strongly intrenched in our front.

July 1st Genl Sheridan accompanied by our Co. scout out in front towards the enemy. Meeting a citizen he informs us that Tullahoma has been evacuated; approaching it we find the town deserted of rebel troops. It is well fortified, but not a good situation for a stand, as it could be easily flanked; some stragglers gave themselves up. Our Division arriving march through the town.

July 3d Genl Sheridan orders the Capt to take our full escort and ride into Winchester ahead of the skirmish line. Reaching the town, we made a dash through its streets. An orderly was sent to recall us, but we were to swift for him and had captured some prisoners. When he reached us, a force of rebel cavalry attempted to cut off our retreat, and might have succeeded if our infantry had not come up just in time to fight them off. Lieut Grow and four of us, separated from the rest and went to the town jail, which was in charge of an old couple, who invited us to dinner, which was then ready; we accepted, and dined with them, for which they refused pay, saying the sight of the stars and stripes was pay enough for them.

July 4th Have gone into camp at Cowan Station, situated near the foot of Cumberland Mountain range; expect to remain here until the rest of the Army comes up, and cross the mountains with forces well in hand. The day has been clear and fine, and it being independence day, a salute was ordered with one of the batteries just before sun down. The guns were fired en battery and they sent forth their terrific music, which echoed and re-echoed from the ravines and mountain sides; clouds gathered in the clear sky. And a terrific clap of thunder sounded over head, and the lightning flashed with the flash of the guns. Down came the rain in a perfect deluge; the storm was precipitated no doubt by the cannonade in a humid atmosphere. The gunners continued to load and fire to the finish the twenty one guns in honor of the day. Exposed to the raging elements and the fearful downpour, which was so unusually heavy, we could but dimly see the battery, though it was but a short distance from our tent.

It seemed as though a contest was raging between the artillery in the clouds and that of our mundane battery. A flash from each gun is followed by flashes of lightning. The roar of our guns is answered by the thunders above, while the echoes from the mountains side, furnished a scene no one could forget: The lightning flashed; the thunder rolled.

The Heavens seemed rent in twain
The guns belched forth their fire and flame,
The thunder roar'd again
Flash after flash from earth and sky;
Nor quenced they them the rain.

Soon after the guns became silent the storm ceased, and the sun went down in a red glory. An officer of the 15th Missouri shot one of his men for some insubordination. The officer was placed under arrest by his Colonel.

July 6th Bridgeport, situated on the Tennessee River, is evacuated by the enemy.

July 7th News has reached us that Vicksburg on the Mississippi River has surrendered to Grant. Another stronghold of the enemy is in our hands. Thus they fall one by one. The news is cheering to our army.

July 12th Five of our orderlies ride outside our picket line in search of blackberries. They got no blackberries, but did get a chase by some rebel cavalry whom they ran on to unexpectedly.

July 14th A squad of our escort accompany A.D.C. Capt [William L.] Mallory into Winchester; after looking the town over, we ride to Deckard [Decherd] Station where our supply of live cattle are hurded, some several thousand in number. The Captain having a requisition for a good bunch of them, we start them out on the road and drive them to our camp at Cowan Station.

July 19th Wm Morse and I, get leave of absence and start on a trip for the top of Cumberland Mountain, the 3d Brigade being camped on a plateau on its top, His Regiment the 42d Ill. and my regt with them. After a pleasant ride and long climb, we reach their camp and take pot luck with our respective Companies, after which we join forces and start back. Thinking to shorten our ride by taking a short cut, instead of following the devious windings of the main road, we turned into the timber. After riding quite a distance we found ourselves in a deep ravine, and completely off our bearings, in fact we were lost. To our right towering up to a great height was a wall reaching to the mountain top; this could be scaled only by wings, and as ours had not yet sufficiently grown, we concluded to pass it by. The sun was nearly at its diernal end and the shaddows swiftly thickening about us in this deep declevity, I suggested that, unless we wanted to play the babies in the wood, we had better make for the nearest high point, and take observations from the western sky, and get our bearings. Dismounting, we led our animals up a steep path, so steep in some places that, our horses all but gave up the struggle. Reaching the top, a good deal fagged, after resting our horses we rode forward to a clearing which gave us a fair view of the western sky just in time to catch the last gleams and take a general course by its uncertain light. We soon found the right road, and at 9 P.M. reached camp.

20th A squad of escort, accompanied Capt [Henry] Hescock (of Hescocks battery [Battery G, 1st

Missouri Light Artillery]) and the Major our topo-
graphical engineer [Francis Mohrhardt] on a tour
of inspection up the mountain. Saw the RR tunnel,
engraved over the rocky arch: Length 2280 feet,
under construction five years, is solid rock throughout its length, at sundown return again.

21st Lakey and I guard some prisoners to Deckard; among them is a young couple, with a ten days
old infant, the mother being about eighteen.

23d A rebel spy is captured while trying to get by
our picket lines. Balcom and I are detailed to guard
him to Winchester and deliver him to Col [William
Truesdail] Truesdale, who is at the head of our
secret service division. We reach there about one
o'clock A.M. and told the sentinal to call up the
Colonel; to him we turned over our prisoner. To our
surprise the Col shook the spies hand heartily, as
an old friend. We learn he is one of our spies and is
loaded with important information. We were given
quarters for the rest of the night and after breakfast
returned to Camp.

Aug 4th I carry a dispatch to Col. Bradley who
commands the brigade on top of the Mountain, then
rode over to Co. C. to see Cal and the boys, who
invite me to supper. A storm was threatening so I
hasten my departure, but before I had rode far, the
clouds settled all around me, and I was riding in the
midst of the storm clouds, and although the sun was
not yet gone down, it became as dark as a "stack of
black cats," as the saying is. The lightning zig-

zagged all through the clouds, on both sides of the road, and the claps of thunder almost split the drum of my ears, such an experience, while it was a great novelty, to be sure, I felt any thing but easy. My steel saber and spurs I was sure would attract the lightning. My horse seemed to partake of my uneasiness, as he trembled at every clap of thunder, I let him have his head, and he went at a sharp gallop. The constant flashes, lit up the misty way. Reaching the brow of the mountain, we were soon below the clouds, and in a drenching rain, which soon penetrated clear to my skin.

However when I struck the level plain, I rode at a sharp run, and soon got to my tent, soaking wet, but glad we were alive. I soon got into a dry suit, and felt none the worse for the drenching.

Aug 5th The camp is broken up, and the army march over the mountain, passing through Tantalon and Anderson. Go into camp at Stevenson Ala.

Aug 7th Capt [A.F.] Stevenson A.D.C. Myself and two others of the escort ride down to the bank of the Tennessee River. By direction I go down to the waters edge, use my hands for a trumpet, call over to the rebel picket line which are on the opposite bank, asking one of them to come over and visit us. Upon my promise that he might return unmolested when he wished, one of them got into a dug-out and paddled over to us. After landing we all sat upon a log for a confab. He informed us his name was Crow, and was a member of the 3d Confederate Cavalry. After a short chat with our enemy, he departed back to the confederate side of the river, and we rode back to Camp.

Aug 12th Morse and I rode over to Anderson to pay a visit to the original Mr Anderson after whom the town was named. The old gentleman was quite talkative, describing to us his large domain. It is so extensive that one can gaze up and down the valley, from his front yard, and the eye can not see the border of his possessions in either direction, while across from mountain to mountain, fading away in the misty distance, does it extend. He can stand upon his door step and exclaim I am monarch of all I survey. It is said to be the largest plantation in the south, and he remarked it would take three days to ride around it.

Sept 1st HeadQuarters moved forward twelve miles to Bridgeport; I rode over to my regiment and took pot luck with bro. Cal.

2d A pontoon bridge, constructed with boats made of frames with canvass drawn over them, planks and stringers formed the flooring; on this we crossed the Tenn. River, and marching ford. five miles, went into camp. But before our teams could cross, the swift current broke the bridge up, and as all our provisions were in the wagons, we made our following three meals on corn taken from the fields and roasted over the fire, our horses feeding on the same, raw however.

Artillery Moves Up

Sept 4th Our Corps march to Racoon, or Sand Mountain, as some call it, and climb its steep road to the top of the range. The climb is so steep, the artillery are compelled to double their teams, that is, use twelve horses to each gun. A long rope is also strung out and a regiment of infantry assist the horses. On reaching the top, I ride over to the brow to take a look at the land scape. The view is a magnificent one. One can see to the north and west miles upon miles of country, streaching out until it is lost in the blue misty atmosphere. Here and there you can see a plantation with its houses and out buildings, which look like toy houses, while a man or animal dwindles down to only a moving object dwarfed by the distance. The river, as it winds along in its serpentine course, looks like a silver thread reflecting the warm rays of the sun, a thing of beauty in the distance. The valley below is full of marching troops, babys in blue they look, with a long bright needle resting upon each one, as the sun reflects from the polished barrel of each gun. Interspersed among the marching pigmies is long lines of army wagons, each with its canvas cover, stretching afar off in the distance, like moving white spots, each drawn by six Jack Rabbits, their long ears and heads look like exclamation points. What a living, moving, picture for some artist to transfer to canvas, with its many colored features. It would take a master hand to do it small justice.

Sept 5th The troops having all gained the summit, we move forward across its level stretch, and down its eastern slope into the valley; reaching Trenton Ga, go into camp. We are now about eighteen miles south of Chattanooga, (the objective point of this campaign) which is in possession of the enemy. An amusing incident occurred today while the Genl. and staff and we orderlies were grouped together on the top of the mountain, sitting on our horses. An artist and reporter who is an attache of our HdQrs. and represents some illustrated paper in the East, rode out a little distance to the brow of the mountain, to get a view of the scenes. He unfortunately stoped his horse directly over a yellow Jackets nest; one of them resenting this, flew up and stung his horse, which made him kick, and bringing his foot down in the middle of the nest stirred up the whole colony, and they swarmed all over the animal, and the A & R. Such a stamping, and kicking, and bucking, as that poor animal went through, snorting, and lashing his tail, until the A & R was pitched off his back landing in the grass. He sprang up, and started on a dead run swinging his arms like a wind mill in a hurry cane, while his horse lay down and tried to roll over to crush his tormentors; the saddle hindered this maneuver, so he got up and took after his master. The General and staff roared with laughter and we joined in the chorus, and it was some time before we recovered. I just imagined if the artist had taken his own picture on the spot, and sent a description to his paper, his fortune would be made.

Sept 7th March through Look-out valley. It is reported that Chattanooga is evacuated.

Sept 10th The army crosses Lookout Valley and ascends Look out Mountain range. Another steep climb. On reaching the top, I rode into some timber and discovered a deep chasm, or depression in the mountain top. An enormous hole with walls of solid rock, oblong in shape, about two hundred yards across its top, and an eighth of a mile long, the walls descend abruptly about sixty or eighty feet down to a smooth sheet of water of unknown depth. The surface as still as death, except at its upper end, where a thin thread of water is runing over an over hanging ledge, breaking into a fine spray before it reaches the surface of the lake; at the lower end I can see a narrow opening between walls of rock, which is no doubt an out let for the lake, when it rises high enough to flow over; a beautiful sheet of water, as the sun shines upon its still surface, its rays penetrating far beneath, until lost in its inky darkness. Altogether it forms a wild scene in nature, and one I shall not soon forget.

Sept 11th Reach Alpine Ga. and camp.

Sept 13th We receive orders to make a retrograde movement to the Northward. It is discovered that Braggs Army is concentrating on the Chickamauga, while our army is fearfully scattered, with long stretches intervening between divisions. If Bragg should attack us now, he could whip us in detail perhaps, if he knows our scattered condition. If he will keep his hands off for a few days, we will be in better condition to cope with him.

Sept 15th The Army is rapidly marching; I am directed by the Genl. to guard the premices of a union family against stragglers. They are making all haste to go north bag and baggage. After our division have passed, I ride forward again.

Sept 16th Reaching the valley through Stevens Gap, a line of battle is formed, expecting an attack, but we were agreeably disappointed as none occurred.

Sept 18th Our division have taken an excellent position, with [Thomas J.] Woods division on our left, and Genl Thomas'es [George H. Thomas] Corps further on but too far away to form an im-

mediate junction. [David S.] Stanleys division is
away south of us, but rapidly marching northward.
Our army faces east, that is the right wing; the left
wing bending round facing more southward.

Sept 19th The morning dawned bright and clear,
and our skirmishers were soon engaged with the
enemy .. slowly our outer lines fall back and take
their places in the line of battle and the main line
on our left become heavily engaged. The roll of
musketry is continuous, gradually coming along our
front, until our (Sheridans) division opens up its
fire. The battle becomes general, as Brigade after
brigade marches up in line of battle, and sends in
their deadly volleys. Battery after battery of artillery, opens up from their elevations in the rear of
the infantry, firing over their heads, into the enemys
ranks. The rebel batteries respond in like manner,
and soon the air is full of flying shells, some passing
beyond our rear, and some bursting over head,
scattering their fragments in every direction.

The wounded are being carried off the field and
down to Craw fish spring, where our field hospital is
located. The Surgeons have their hands fully occupied. Many of our batteries had to change position
or cease firing, their shells cut off many limbs from
the trees, which endangered our own men. The
fighting is mostly in the open timber. The roll of
musketry is incessant, as our lines change position
for a more advantageous one, pressing the rebels
back, as we push gradually forward. Bradleys bri-

gade drive the rebels in a charge, and gain a slight elevation, about 4. P.M. and hold it. But were obliged to lay down, to escape a sweeping fire from a rebel battery and a strong force of infantry. To the northward of our position could be heard the steady roll of musketry, and the play of batteries, which indicated a heavy engagement going on there. From the prisoners we captured, it is learned, that Bragg is expecting some heavy reinforcements at any moment, said to be [James] Longstreets corps from the rebel army in the east, which news has a depressing effect on our men. So far, neither side could claim any decided advantage, as night came on the firing gradually ceased. The losses on both sides are heavy. No camp fires are lighted, as that would expose our position to the enemy. They also take the same precaution. Soon after night spread its mantle over the scene, hiding from view the worst features of the bloody strife. It set in cold and frosty. Fires would have added some comfort to the weary soldiers, as they lay down upon the cold ground to seek much needed rest. Four of us lay under the friendly branches of a large tree, lying close together for mutual warmth. I looked up at the clear blue sky, thinking over the events of the day, and watched the bright stars, and the queen of night, the round silver moon, resting in peace up there in the blue vault, of Heaven, while its light reflects down upon the upturned white cold faces, of hundreds of the dead, motionless they lay all over the field; they are at peace. At the roll of the drum, in the morning, calling to arms again, to renew the strife, they will not respond, but sleep peacefully on through the deadly strife to follow. No doubt the wires have flashed the news to the north of the great battle being fought, down here in Georgia, and mothers, wives and sweet hearts, are praying for the safety of their loved ones. Of those who escaped today, how many will face tomorrow. Thinking of these things I fall a sleep; some time after midnight I was awakened by a noise over in the enemys lines. Listening I could hear the rumbling of a moveing train; Longstreet with his corps of twenty or more thousand men are come. Many a heart will sink at this unwelcome sound. The disembarking of the troops can be plainly heard in the clear silent air. I soon fall asleep again and finish the night. At the first dawn of light in the east the whole army is up, and breaking their fast, expecting every moment the enemy's attack.

CHAPTER V

The first day of fighting at Chickamauga follows a day of marching and countermarching by both armies. By first light of September 19, a large part of Bragg's army is west of Chickamauga Creek. And on the 18th, Longstreet's first three brigades (commanded by John B. Hood) arrive from Virginia. Bragg first plans to attack Crittenden—the Union left—but finds that Rosecrans has been able to move Thomas's corps behind Crittenden. The fighting on the 19th has been called "bitter, prolonged, and inconclusive," with Thomas repulsing the major Confederate attacks. Longstreet arrives in person that night, and it is decided to continue against the Union left in the morning. Thomas holds firm, but because of a misunderstanding a gap is opened on the Union right and as Union troops (including Sheridan's men) move into the gap they are irresistibly attacked by Longstreet. Shattered by this attack, Sheridan retreats from the field through McFarland's Gap; Rosecrans, along with McCook and Crittenden, also move off, leaving Thomas in command with orders to withdraw. But supported by Brigadier General James B. Steedman's troops from General Granger's reserve corps, Thomas holds against all Confederate attacks, earning the nickname "Rock of Chickamauga." That evening, with the help of Sheridan and others who have returned to the field, Thomas withdraws to Rossville. Private Smith is in the gap during Longstreet's attack and helps ambush a column of the 24th Alabama; he then makes his way to the rear of Thomas's position and finally to Chattanooga.

Meanwhile, Bragg closes in on Chattanooga, occupying Missionary Ridge, the valley between that ridge and Lookout Mountain, and the mountain itself. From these positions the Confederates can prevent supplies from entering the town either by water or over the main road from the west. Rosecrans is thus forced to depend upon a roundabout route from the railroad at Stevenson, Alabama. And so the Confederates sit down to starve out the Union troops.

Smith is sent by General Sheridan on a dangerous mission to Bridgeport, Alabama, and after a long and circuitous ride arrives safely. Later, following orders from Sheridan, Smith asks rebel pickets to cease firing, and tells them that the Union pickets will follow suit; both sides comply.

Meanwhile, command changes are made and plans are being worked out to break out of the city. General Ulysses S. Grant assumes command of the troops in the West; strong reinforcements, including General Hooker with two corps—the 11th and the 12th—arrive from Meade's army in the East and from Vicksburg comes General Sherman with the 15th and 17th corps.

On the 23rd of October, General Grant arrives and, on the 27th Generals Turchin and Hazen capture Brown's Ferry, while Hooker moves from Bridgeport straight east until he reaches the ferry. As a result of this maneuver, a new and shorter route of supply is opened, but it is a rough, man-killing route over Raccoon Mountain, quickly named the "cracker line."

November 23rd sees Orchard Knob captured by Wood and Sheridan; Sherman begins to attack the north end of Missionary Ridge as Grant opens his offensive; on the 24th Hooker attacks and captures Lookout Mountain, the so-called "Battle Above the Clouds," even though the battle is fought far down the mountainside, and the clouds are a combination of gun smoke and mist.

20th This is the Sabbath day, and is bright and clear. Each and every one devours his meal in haste, anticipating trouble at any moment, knowing that the enemy has received an army of reinforcements during the past night. It is with great surprise, that moment after moment passes away and not a shot from either side, breakes the silence. An hour, two hours have come and gone, still no sign is manifested, what does it mean? Col. Bradley of our 51st while commanding the brigade yesterday was badly wounded; there is no braver officer then he. If he recovers, he is entitled to a star. We are all in the Saddle at HdQrs. Genls. Sheridan, [Alexander McDowell] McCook and Rosecrans are together discussing the situation. Feeling thirsty I rode forward, down to a spring, dismounted and laying flat, drink there from. My horse doing like wise, just then the ball opened; just to our left the rifles began to crack. I sprang up and mounted, and found our skirmishing line retreating, while the enemy were rapidly advancing and their bullets cutting the brush all around me. I rode back to where I had left the Genls and escort, but they had disappeared. The battle was on in earnest now; the continous roll of musketry, and boom of cannons was enough to break the crack of doom. Our division moves to the left and swing towards the rear leaving a gap, which is hastily filled, with [John T.] Wilders mounted infantry on foot, who with their spencer rifles, seven shooters, play havoc in the ranks of the rebel lines, and cause them to swing to their right. Wilders men are short of ammunition, and are compelled to pull out Northward also. All this is accomplished in a few moments; the rapid retreat of our forces towards the left, leaves me cut off from them with the rebel army between us. On the knoll where I am, is two

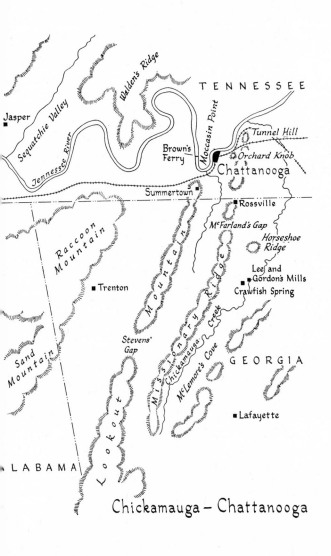

Chickamauga – Chattanooga

guns of a battery, with no ammunition except one charge, a shell; coming out of the woods is many stragglers, who without any officers, are in a demoralized condition. Not knowing which way to go, Lieut [James] Boyd of Co D of the 51st came up with a few men in charge. I rode down to the road and directed the men to where Boyd was on top of the knoll. Most of them went up, a few went on southward, paying no heed to me. And no doubt they were captured. A force of two hundred was then collected on the knoll, and put themselves under Boyd, who directed them all to lay low and await events. If they would stay together there was a fighting chance to escape. The battle was raging fiercer than ever North of us. The whole forces on both sides were in the struggle. Having our little force in hand none to soon, for we had caught sight of a rebel force coming from their main army no doubt sent back to gather the many stragglers from our army; they were about equal in force to ours. Marching towards our knoll, they could see only our two cannon and the men who were in charge, the artillerymen, and myself, I being mounted, and just back of the infantry who were all concealed by laying down. Boyd passed the word among them, to keep down until he gave the word. On the rebels came, and letting off a yell, they charged on a run; reaching the foot of the rising ground, they fired a volley. Sitting on my horse side ways to them, my horse dancing a jig in his excitement, the bullets

Wet Going for the Horse Artillery

flew all around me, one passing through my hair on the back of my neck. The artillerymen wheeled the gun around, and fired their last shot. Boyd sprang up with his two hundred men, who sent in a volley at short range, and ordered a charge; the rebs were taken by surprise, and scattered in all directions. Down the hill we went, and so close to us were they, that we captured a squad of prisoners, including their color guard and flag. They proved to be a part of the 24th Alabama regiment. Boyd tore the flag from its staff and folding it up, put it inside his blouse. Thus was the over confident enemy defeated[1].

[1] The report of Colonel N. N. Davis, commanding the 24th Alabama Infantry, has a slightly different version of this incident (*O.R.*, I, 30, part 2, p. 346): "After moving forward about 400 or 500 yards through the woods, the regiment entered an open field, through which it continued to advance briskly for some distance up a gentle slope, and immediately upon arriving upon the crest of the hill the enemy opened

Such incidents are liable to occur, during any great battle. My revolver being empty I reloaded, and shortly after turned towards the west, to Look-out range, as my only hope of escape was to circumvent the left flank of the rebel Army. Boyd with his men started also, and the two cannon followed, as no doubt another force of rebels might come, and a

---

upon us a heavy fire of musketry and artillery. The order having been previously given to guide upon the regiment on the right, in order to do this the regiment was compelled to oblique to the right, which threw the right wing into the woods skirting the field. After moving forward a short distance, the regiment came under a heavy cross-fire from the left besides a severe fire from the front. It being discovered that we were being flanked on our left, the order was given to fall back, which was immediately obeyed.

In this charge the regiment suffered severely, both in killed and wounded. Capt. W. J. O'Brien was mortally wounded while gallantly leading his company forward, and Capt. B. S. Chamberlain severely wounded while leading on his men. Lieutenant Cooper was dangerously wounded while some distance in advance of his regiment. The color bearer, Sergt. George W. Moody, receiving a severe wound, dropped the colors, which was not discovered until after the regiment was rallied. Lieutenant Young, with 4 men, immediately volunteered to bring them off the field, but they could not be found. It is reported that Sergt. George B. Ackerman, of Company G, was seen with the colors in hand going toward the enemy's lines, and it is supposed he deserted, as he has not been heard from since."

Lt. Colonel Samuel B. Raymond, then commanding the 51st Illinois, credits the capture of this battle flag to a different officer: "During the engagement of this day Lieutenant [Thomas H.] Cummings, of Company D, assisted by a squad of men representing several other regiments, captured the battleflag of the Twenty-fourth Alabama Regiment." *O.R.*, I, 30, part 1, p. 1057.

larger one too, perhaps. I soon came to the road, leading to Chattanooga. Before I left the field, which was strewn with the dead, both blue and gray, I saw a dead comrade, with a full haversack beside him; having no provisions of my own, and knowing he had no further use for rations, I took it with me, not knowing when I would be able to get where our provisions were. The road was lined with our wagon trains, for miles, all hastening towards Chattanooga and safety, with no guards to protect them. I thought how easy it would be for the rebs to capture and destroy the whole outfit. About dusk I came to a field of ripe corn, my horse being as nearly famished as myself. Neither of us having had a bite since early morning, I conclude to rest a bit, gathering an armful of corn for my horse, and while he is refreshing the inner horse, I investigate my haversack with a view to refreshing the inner man. I find some bacon and hard tack, also some new potatoes. The poor fellow back there on the field, of death, dreamed not that he was providing for a comrade when he filled his sack. The fighting is still going on east of where I sit, but will cease when night sets fairly in. When our meal was over, I again started forward guided by the sounds of battle and soon got to the rear of our army and find them holding a line in conjunction with Genl. Thomas troops, who are behind breastworks, which with flanks turning back on either side form a sort of horse shoe shape. I reach our division or what is left of it about midnight and soon find the General, some of the escort and officers, several of the escort are missing. My bunk mate Wm Morse among them, Brig Genl [William H.] Lytle is killed and many line officers. Thomas has held his position all the after noon, against repeated assaults from the enemy. Every charge they made they were hurled back again, only to attack again. This is the rallying point of the rest of our army. The second days battle is over, and while the enemy may look upon it as a victory, or partially so it has been a dear one, costing thousands of lives, and we still hold the fort. If Thomas, with his great determination of character, had not held his position against the great odds hurled against him, time after time, saving thus a rallying point for our shattered divisions, the day would have been lost and the enemy victorious. And the disaster to our army would have ended in a rout, with perhaps thousands of our men becoming prisoners. The enemy's loss must be greater than ours, they being the attacking party throughout the day, every repulse cost them dearly.

Sept 22d By a masterly retreat, the army is within the defences around Chattanooga, and the lines of defence are being strengthened at every point, with the Tennessee River forming a curve northward from Lookout Mountain, forming a natural protection for our rear, our position is safe. The enemy have taken position upon the heights of Mission Ridge and Lookout Mountain, facing us. And in the valley below.

Sept 26th During the night just past, a company of the 3d Ind. Cav. rode out-side our picket lines, and when they came up to the rebel pickets, made a dash into their camp, creating a small panic among the surprised enemy. Makeing a wide circle, they came back, and coming up to a diferent part of our picket line, were fired on as they aproached, but were identified before any one was hit, or hurt.

Oct 4th Procuring a pass, I cross the river, and pay a visit to our field hospital. Many of my regiment[2] are here wounded, some have died from their wounds, I find Geo Yonker, a member of G. Co. from my old town Kankakee. He has several wounds, but is slowly recovering. [James C.] Bowen of my Co. has a fearful hip wound, and can not recover. The tents are full of wounded men. They seem to be receiving the best of care. It is a sad sight, these helpless men laid low, by the relentless fate of war.

Oct 9th Capt Powell and a squad of us, ride to the top of Andersons Ridge, and visit Capt Card[3], who has organized a Co. of East Tennesseans, with whom we take pot luck, and return to camp after midnight.

Oct 11th Our rations are growing uncomfortably short, our nearest supply station is Stevenson Ala,

[2]The 51st Illinois lost 149 men at the battle of Chickamauga: 2 officers, 16 men killed; 4 officers, 89 men wounded; 1 officer and 37 men captured or missing.

[3]This was doubtless James Card, a civilian who acted as a spy for General Sheridan. See P. H. Sheridan, *Personal Memoirs* (New York: Charles L. Webster & Company, 1888, 2 volumes), Volume I, pp. 206–7, 212–13, 251–52.

some eighty miles distant by the only route open to us, via Sequachee [Sequatchie] Valley. Our foraging parties are bringing in corn from the nearest point in the valley some thirty miles over the Mountains. This is issued to us, for breakfast dinner and supper, also for our horses, with whom we divide. We manage our share after this fashion: with a nail we punch our tin plates full of holes and used the rough side for a grater; after a good deal of patience and hard work, the corn is grated into coarse meal, then mixed with water and salt, is baked over hot coals in other tin plates. This we relish with a diminutive piece of bacon and parched corn coffee, when regular coffee is not forth coming. The rebel cavalry are raiding the valley and cutting off our supplies, burning our wagons with both rations and ammunition.

Oct 13th I receive orders to report to Genl. Sheridan, who directs me to proceed to Stevenson Ala, and order all our division teams, together with those belonging to HdQrs. to pack on all the supplies the wagons will hold and start them to the front. I must make the trip alone, and with the best dispatch consistant with safety &c; I dont relish this trip of eighty miles, over a strange route, and through the valley where the enemy are making their raids, but to receive an order, the only thing to do is to obey it.

Oct 14th I am up at day break, and while one of our mess is getting my breakfast, I give my faithful horse a good feed and rubbing down. After breakfast strap my blanket and rubber poncho to my

Saddle, bid the boys good by, while they wish me a safe journey, for there is a chance of my not getting through without some trouble, and some risk of meeting enemys who may cut my trip short. And the boys are depending on my success for their future grub. With a piece of hoe cake and a slice of bacon in my haversack, I mount my steed and begin my long ride. Crossing the river, I strike the road northward at an easy canter, armed only with my revolver and saber. My revolver is a long navy, and will shoot as accurate and as far as a carbine. About noon it commenced to rain; without stopping I unsling my poncho, and putting my head through the opening in the middle, let the ends fall over my saddle, blanket and tops of my boots, thus I kept comparatively dry. About 4 P.M. or shortly after, it commenced to grow dark, and I reached the foot of Andersons Ridge, and knowing where Captain Card was encamped, on its top, I made all haste to reach it, and arrived none to soon, for it was dark as pitch. But the light from his fires guided me, and after a challenge from the picket I was welcomed and a hot supper set before me, my horse sheltered and fed in one of the shanties. Capt Card and his men seemed to be well supplied with fresh meat and corn bread &c. which I relished very much. And after my all days ride waited for no second invitation to turn into one of their bunks and was soon in the land of dreams.

Oct 15th At daybreak I got out of my comfortable berth, and attending to my horse, had breakfast with the Captain, who gave me some particulars as to my route up the valley. As he knew the country all over that section, it stood me well in hand. Said he did not think that any of [Joseph] Wheelers Cavalry was in the valley as they had just made a raid and would likely not linger there for fear troops would be sent after him; this was encouraging news if true. So I mounted and sped away on my way feeling no apprehension. Crossing the crown of the ridge, I rode down into the valley and turned westward; the roads were heavy and muddy from the rain, that still came down now and then, in showers. The solitude was unbroken as I rode along hour after hour covering the miles as fast as the nature of the road would admit, thinking over many things but always with a sharp eye to the front. Late in the afternoon, I came to a dwelling which set back from the road a short distance, and looked some what promising, and as the houses along my route were many miles apart, and the night coming on with a promise of heavy rain, I concluded to make a halt, and put up for the night, if the people would keep me. Dismounting I hitched my tired animal to the fence, and went up to the door which stood invitingly open under the porch, And I could smell preparations for supper. A man came out to meet me, I asked him if he would shelter me and my horse for the night, and he answered without hesitation "yes," and showed me the way to the log barn in the rear, where I led my horse. Stripping the animal of his saddle and bridle, I turned him into an empty stall, and gave him a good grooming, then fed and watered him. My host led the way into the house, and with a basin of well water I gave myself a good wash, using home made soft soap, which was hardened into cakes, by some process known to the female portion of the family. Supper being ready I was invited to partake. Gathered about the board was mine host (whose name I learn is Holloway) his wife and two grown up daughters, both good looking damsels. Mr Hollaway is past middle age, and said he was a Union man, and had a son in the federal Army, but I judged from his conversation, he was like many others of the natives, astride the fence, he was union to Union men and confederate to the rebels as occasion required, for which I did not blame him if he wants to remain in peace by his fire side. Being tired and sleepy I did not linger long after supper, but requested to be shown to my bed. He took me out on the front poarch and into a small room which was a shed like affair with a low slanting roof, a sort of lean-to as it is called. There was a high bed which nearly filled the whole space, a chair, and small stand upon which he deposited a very diminutive candle, and left me. I examined the door and found no sort of fastening, so placed the chair against it, and got my clothes off. Placing my revolver under my pillow, doused the glim and got into bed, which proved to be an old fashioned feather affair into which I sank with every prospect of enjoying the unusual luxury, and the music of the patter of the rain falling upon the shingles soon put me to sleep. Some time during the night I woke up with a feeling of something pressing the clothes against me, and putting my hand out to feel what it might be, put it into a small lake of water; the rain was coming down on the roof in a deluge, and every hollow in the top of the bed was full it having leaked through the crevices in the shingles. Raising the covering, it went off on the floor, buckets full of it; turning over I was off to sleep again. There being no window in this shanty to let in the morning light, I did not awake until I was called. Getting into my clothes. which were not any too dry from the leaky roof, I attended to my horse, and went in to breakfast, after which I thanked my host for his hospitality, that being the only coin I possessed (as I had drawn no pay for months), I mounted and resumed my way. I reached the place where the rebs had captured a long wagon train that was on its way to Chattanooga loaded with supplies; every wagon had been set on fire, and totaly consumed nothing remained but a heap of black ashes and the iron, and I counted ninety of these, which indicated the number destroyed. Reaching the big Sequachee [Sequatchie] River I found it nearly out of its banks and entirely impassable; usually it is fordable, but the recent rain had made it a raging torrent. Some distance to my left on a piece of rising ground I saw a double log house, and rode to it. I met its owner who greeted me with a pleasant smile and a how-da. I told him I was going to Stevenson, and asked if there was any way to cross the river. He said there was no way, as all the fords were in the same condition as this one, but if it cleared up and stopped raining, it would subside as quickly as it had risen, by tomorrow perhaps I could cross it. In the meantime I was welcome to stay with him and wait. Thinking of the boys in camp, waiting for their rations, I was loath to delay my journey, but seeing no other alternative, concluded to wait. He said his name was Rogers, and was ex sheriff of that County, and a sound Union man. He had a good sized crib of corn on the place and all the surroundings looked encouraging towards feed for man and beast. I was introduced to Mrs Rogers, a portly old lady, and all the rest of the family from the four year old, up the graduated steps in ages to about eighteen, the eldest being a boy whose physical structure was very slim and mostly pointed Heavenward. All the intermediate steps being girls from seventeen down, the two oldest girls looked robust and rosy. I was invited to make myself at home; being ushered into the family room (There being only two in the dwelling) I found it contained mostly beds four of them, including one which slid under a high one, after the fashion of the one I and Cal. occupied when we were youngsters; there was a long bench in front of an enormous old fashioned fire place, and a couple of raw hide bottom chairs. Every thing was neat and clean. Mr R and myself talked war, until supper time, when we all repaired to the kitchen, crossing an open gallery covered by the peak roof which joined the two log houses together. I was hungry, and did full justice to the fried ham, bacon biscuit and corn bread and black coffee, no milk or sugar. The good wife's apologized for the absence of these; I told her, that a soldier seldom had any sugar, and milk was always a stranger.

After supper we gathered around the cheerful fire of blazing logs in the family room. I was a matter of great curiosity to the younger fry, and the older ones, especially the girls, seemed to regard me as a specimen from yankee dom; during the lapses in the conversation I was pondering the question of the sleeping arrangements with some diffidence, but conclude to await developments, and take things easy. The only light in the room was that of the fire, and when I began to nod a little, Mr R suggested I could retire to the corner bed. I proceeded to do so, But with some embarrassment, as I was not used to disrobing before a whole family, or rather behind them; however I finally got between the sheets, and the young man followed suit, getting in behind me. Then the old lady banked up the fire, covering it with the ashes, and the room became dark as Egypt. The rest of the family were soon settled for the night, and I retired to the land of dreams. At the first dawn of day I awoke, and found the room deserted, every body was up and gone except the two youngsters in the trundle bed, so I soon got into my wardrobe and joined them. It had rained nearly all night, and a glance at the river, showed it was still higher than the day previous. I enquired of Mr R if there was such a thing as a boat so I might cross and swim my horse; he said there was none any where that he knew of, and if there was, it would be risky to use it, and said I might as well stay another day. Regreting the delay, I concluded his advice was sound; every meal I sat down to made me think of the boys in camp, who were grating their corn, and feeding on hoe cake.

Oct 17th The river is still on a boom, with poor prospects of its getting lower or back to its normal condition; chafing under my enforced inactivity, about noon I espied a force of engineers on the opposite bank, with a train of wagons, loaded with pontoon boats, composed of wooden ribs and canvas covers, and I rejoiced at the sight, knowing that in two or three hours, they would have a pontoon bridge built. Getting my horse ready I thanked my host for his hospitality and hardly waiting for the last plank to be laid, I crossed over and rode upon my way rejoicing, passing through Jasper at a gallop, and at dusk reached battle creek, and was greatly surprised and pleased to find here encamped, the other half of the old scouts, from whom we had separated in Nashville, just before the Tenn. campaign. The boys gave me a welcome and supper, and I staid over night with them, pleasantly talking over old times.

Oct 18th I got up before day light, and fed my horse and had breakfast, and was on the road just as the light began to show in the east, And soon reached Stevenson, and among the wilderness of wagons found our Hdqr wagon master, and delivered my orders. He said all his teams were loaded to the bows, and only waiting for orders. He gave the order to his teamsters at once, and soon the whole line was en-route for Chattanooga with a force of guards sufficient to protect them from all raids from the enemy.

I listened to the farewell address of Genl Rosecrans, which he gave in front of his HdQrs, and also some remarks made by Genl [Joseph] Hooker. He having recently came from the army of the Potomac, was listened to with much attention by the troops. Personally, Rosecrans or old Rosa as the boys call him, is well liked, but having in mind the mismanagement of the recent campaign, or the latter part of it, together with the disastrous battle of Chickamauga, which was all but lost, they do not feel altogether kindly disposed toward him. But the encouraging report that Genl Grant is coming to take charge of affairs, makes the army feel more hopeful for the future.

Oct 24th After breakfast I mount my faithful steed and turn our faces towards Chattanooga. There has been established a line of Currier posts, within short riding distances of each other on a shorter line to Chattanooga, so I conclude to follow this, from post to post, but find it a rough road to travel, up hill and down dale, over mountains and through valleys; at night fall I put up at one of the posts.

Oct 27th I arrived in "C" early this morning, without incident, and find the Genl has moved into town and occupies one of the large houses for HdQrs. I report myself, and told him the teams would arrive in a short time; he thanked me, and I go and find the boys who are housed in a wing of the house, taking things easy. The Rebels have not been idle. They are planting a siege battery of heavy guns, on the extreme northern point of Lookout Mountain, and our HdQrs is in a straight line from the muzzles of their guns, about three miles intervening. We may look for some music from them when they are ready to sing; they can drop their big shells right down upon us.

Oct 28th Our mess cook has erected an out door table, using four forked sticks for standards, drove in the ground with cross poles on top, and planks laid on, to which we stand up and eat our rations, which are plentiful in quantity and variety, since our wagon trains have come in. Today, while we were eating our dinner, a cloud of smoke puffed up from the crown of Point Look out, followed by a report, and presently the screech of a big shell as big as a water bucket came over our heads and struck over near the river at the north end of town. Then another followed and exploded in town on the hill, with a tremendous roar. The rebs are getting their range. This is continued at intervals of every half hour, and one or two of the monsters fell and exploded uncomfortably near our head quarters. After a time we became used to it, and hardly noticed them. Its a good thing for us, they have only two of these guns; with a dozen of such like pieces they would soon lay the town in ashes or splinters. We are unable to respond, for the want of guns of heavy calibre, or an elevation high enough to reach them.

Oct 29th A sharp skirmish took place up Look out valley. Hooker is over there, no particulars have come.

Nov 1st Out beyond our defence line of works, a short distance have been dug a chain of rifle pits, which are occupied during day time by pickets, fac-

River Picket Becomes Gunboat Target

ing a belt of timber occupied by the enemy picket line. They use convenient trees for shelter, shots are exchanged when either side show any part of their anatomy for a mark, and during the past few days several of our men have been hit. During the forenoon Genl Sheridan with three of his staff officers and a dozen orderlies, rode out side our breastworks, and near the rifle pits. The General turned to me (I happened to be near him, though not the nearest) and said "Smith, you dismount and go out between the lines within talking distance of the rebels, and tell them If they will cease firing our pickets will be ordered to stop also, as it accomplished nothing to murder each other." I dismounted, one of the boys held my horse, and as I started on my errand, the firing ceased on both sides. I did not relish my Job just then, for perhaps I might become a target for some smart aleck among the rebs, at close range. However I advanced until some one of the staff cried halt, and then I said my little speech to the rebel pickets. It wasent very long to be sure, but under the circumstances, it seemed an age, to me, and when I got back to our lines I felt greatly relieved. The Genl smiled a little as I mounted again, and we rode back to quarters, but it had served its purpose. The pickets quit firing at each other from thence forward. Thinking of the matter later I was surprised that no Jonny reb took a shot at me, for previously, they had shot at every thing in blue.

Nov 13th I witnessed the execution of two men today. They had been courtmarshalled for bounty jumping and desertion; there cases must have been of an aggravating nature. Mr Lincoln did not use his prerogative of clemency and commute their sentence to imprisonment. They were both shot in the head, and died instantly.

22d Sergt Parks and Darling went foraging over in Sequachee Valley, and returned with turkeys and chickens for our thanksgiving dinner.

23d Genl O[liver] O Howard (the one armed Genl) passed through our lines with the 11th Corps, drove the enemy from our front back towards Mission Ridge and intrenched themselves well into the former line occupied by the enemy.

24th Genl Hookers Army attacked Look Out Mountain from his side of the western valley. The enemy fell back, retreating up the slope and around the face of the mountain under point-Look-out. From our camp we could see the battle as it progressed. A battery was situated on Moccasin point just across the river from the Mountain, sent some shells among the rebs, but could not elevate the guns enough to do much execution. The battle continued until a large force on both sides were engaged. The smoke from their guns formed great clouds, which settled upon the combatants, and hid them from our view, a virtual battle among the clouds. The engagement continued long after night fall, and we could see the flash of the rifles from both friend and foe, which looked like a swarm of fire flys in the distant darkness. Word has come in that the rebs have spiked their big guns on point lookout, and retreated, so Hookers movements were successful.

Chapter VI

Wherein Smith watches the Battle of Missionary Ridge with General Sheridan. When Sherman's troops attack the north end of Missionary Ridge but make no headway and Hooker fails to reach his objective as scheduled, Grant orders Thomas to capture the Confederate works lowest down on the ridge, and then halt. In a straight frontal assault the first line is captured, but the troops do not halt; instead they stream upward, carrying all before them, out of the control of their officers. During the march towards the first line of trenches, Smith gets a fresh horse for Sheridan, and then is the only one of the staff to go on to the top of the ridge with the General. Returning to Chattanooga, Smith leaves for Knoxville and east Tennessee, where Longstreet is besieging Burnside's soldiers. Longstreet has been sent from Chattanooga on November 4 to attack Burnside, but Burnside successfully withdraws into Knoxville; on the 29th, after waiting more than a week for additional cavalry, Longstreet launches his attack on Knoxville by assaulting Fort Sanders, and is repulsed. Meanwhile (November 26, 1863) Grant has ordered Sherman (15th Corps) and Granger (4th Corps) to relieve Knoxville, but as they approach, Longstreet lifts the siege and moves off to the east. Sherman then returns to Chattanooga and Granger enters Knoxville.

Burnside is relieved by General John G. Foster on December 11; Smith marches with several friends to Knoxville, and near here serves as Sheridan's messenger. Here, too, Smith re-enlists and is now entitled to be called a ''veteran volunteer.'' As a reward for re-enlistment he is given a thirty-day furlough; after a slow trip to Chattanooga and an exploring session in the mountains near the town, he is mustered in again and starts for Illinois. After spending time in Chicago and Kankakee, he leaves for Providence, Rhode Island. After ten days with his sister Mary's friends he starts back for the Army of the Cumberland.

Nov 25th I am on duty with the General! The day is bright and clear. Several corps and Division commanders ride out together to an elevation which gives a good view of Mission Ridge for miles up and down our front. The line of breastworks with their head logs strung along its top, and bristling with numerous black mouthed cannon, the steep sides of the ridge, with another line of works strung along its base, would seem to make the rebel defenses all but impregnable, to a direct attack. Yet this is what is contemplated. Genl [William T.] Sherman with the 15th & 17th Corps on our left has already begun an attack, and is pounding away on our extreme left. In front of the center where we are, there is an open field some half to three quarters of a mile leading up to the ridge, bordered just in our front by a belt of timber, in front of which, in plain view of the enemy our troops are marching to the left, seeming with a view to reinforce Sherman. But this maneuver is only to deceive the enemy, for after marching some distance, the troops go into the timber, and counter march back to their old position; we can see the

A Field Gun Changes Hands

rebels are moving some of their forces to their right as they march along within their works. When all is ready the order is given to advance. Moving out in regimental or semi brigade front, with intervals, and lapping each other, when our lines are well on their way, the enemy open up their artillery all along their line, and the shot and shell is rained down upon the field. As our division is crossing through this hail of shot and shell, I ride out with the Genl who has only one staff officer, Capt [J.S.] Ransom and two or three orderlies. I can see up and down the field as far as it extends, and owing to the formation of the troops, it seems literally covered with them; the army appears much greater than it is. Its a most beautiful sight, but one can not contemplate it long, as the troops finding the rebel shot are falling among them they break into a double quick to the sooner gain the base of the ridge, as the enemy can not depress their guns enough for a direct fire. In crossing the field many of the rebel shots made gaps in some of the regiments. The lower line of works are captured with a rush, and all who occupy them are captured. If they tried to climb the ridge they were sure of being shot so they stayed in their trenches and surrendered. Genl Sheridans horse was wounded in his forefoot and he told me to bring up his big black horse. I made a dash across the field, and returned with his horse, which I rode, as mine was nearly blowed. I exchanged again, and he sent one of the other orderlies back with the wounded animal. The troops having rested, started to climb the steep sides of the ridge. An aide having been sent to Genl [Gordon] Granger for further orders, came back with a suggestion that the troops be recalled if it was judged expedient. By this time they were half way up the ridge, every regiment had lost its organization, and were all massed in a sort of triangle with the point upwards, about every flag of our division was struggling to reach the top first, every man for himself. Now and then a flag would fall, its bearer being shot, but it appeared in an instant held by the next soldier. The Genl said, let them go, they will be over in five minutes, and so it proved, a dozen flags went over the works. The men following nothing could stop their rush, the rebels deserted their guns and fled; hundreds of them, staying a moment too long were captured. An old log hut standing just to the left to where our division went over, was occupied by Genl Bragg and his staff; they had barely time to mount and ride away. Some of the rebel guns were turned upon their retreating ranks, and shots sent after them. More than fifty guns were captured; when we reached the top of the ridge, my horse was about ready to drop from the unusual hard work he had done, So I took the harness off of a big white horse that had belonged to one of the rebel batteries, and put my saddle on him, turning mine loose to shift for himself, and that was the last I ever saw of my good old friend. But this animal is the tallest piece of horse flesh in four counties. I must look like a fly on a ridge pole, and feel as though I am astride of a small mountain, but there is no time for comments, our troops are in full cry after the retreating enemy and it is growing dark. Lieut Wyman is killed; he was a Sergt in the old Powells Scouts, but had recently recd. a commission; he lay half way up the ridge with his sword still grasped in his dead hand. The wounded are being conveyed to Chattanooga. I ride back to head quarters on my big white horse. He gets over the ground in great shape with his long legs, but he wont do for my service. I took him to the Quarter-Master who was glad to get the animal for artillery service, and he gave me one in exchange, one more suited for my work.

Nov 27th Sergt. L L Parks who has been my bunk mate for some time past, in fact since Wm Morse was made a prisoner at Chickamauga, Rec'd a Lieutenant's commission today, and is assigned to a Co in the 13th US colored troops, and is ordered to report to Nashville at once to join his troop.

28th Four days rations issued to our corps and orders to march with all haste to the relief of Knoxville East Tenn. Reb Genl Longstreet with his corps is making for that point. Gen [Ambrose E. Burnside] Burnsides is located there with a force rather slim for such an emergency. When I had rode a few miles on our way, the horse, which our div. Sergeon Maj [David J. Griffith] Griffith rode, went lame. By request I exchanged animals with him, and returned

Army Smith Re-shoes Horses

to Chattanooga to await orders. Balcom, Dink, and two others of the escort having been left behind in charge of HdQrs. I joined them; our black smith Frazier is also there. I conclude to take life easy, and put in my time writing up my diary and correspondence to date.

Dec 2d Recd orders to follow and join our command. I received a new horse from the Post Qr master. Balcom, Dink, Stull, Frazier and myself set out after breakfast, cross the river and strike the Loudon road. Frazier is a Dutchman of the most pronounced type and is mounted on a sorry specimen of the Army mule. Said mule evidently has a charactor of his own, which taken together with his excentric master, affords us considerable amusement. For instance his muleship is a very small specimen as mules go, while Frazier is built upon a long lank pattern; in consequence his feet all but touch the ground. The animal having seen his best days, is not in condition to do any great amount of marching. So when an idea enters his mule head that he wants a rest, he just stops dead short in his tracks, and no amount of persuasion can move him therefrom. And Frazier has to dismount and lead him, and so there is an under standing established between them! After a time when he thinks the mule has forgotten he was tired, he again mounts and this operation is repeated every few miles. We throw chaff at him, which he takes good naturedly. Balcom called out to him, "Frazier your mule is tired." he looked at us in all earnestness, and said, "Dont say dot poys, der 'tam mule vil hear you, und I haf to valk," which made us roar at him. "Dont laugh poys, tis mule he gets mat." At night fall we put up at a citizens house, by the roadside. Supper was gotten for us, and we enjoyed some feather beds for the night, except Frazier who curled himself up in his blanket and lay on the floor in front of the fire place, and he was soon snoring with tuneful regularity.

Dec 3d We are up at break of day, and after attending to our horses, had breakfast. We were soon on the road again. Fraziers mule soon demonstrated that his memory was good, for he insisted upon being led when his tired spell came on. Frazier is a man of patience as we can testify, but by and by he concluded that patience had ceased to be a virtue. About noon we stoped at a house for dinner. Frazier asked our host if he had any thing on four feet to trade for a fine mule. He looked the mule over, and said he had a horse to trade. Said he was a little thin, but would improve with plenty of corn. "Shust you trot dot horse out" said F. So the horse was produced at once, he was a sorry looking frame, and as much flesh on his ribs, as a rail fence could show; looked to be at least a quarter of a hundred in age; his points were many and stuck out in all directions. F. was too delighted to note these things, a horse was a horse to him, and he winked at us as he transferred his saddle, "He ist your mule Mr." at the same time he gave the animal a kick in the ribs by way of parting salute. "Now poys I am wid you," and he mounted. The horse did show more vigor than we expected. We made about thirty two miles during the day; at night fall, we stoped with an old lady named Jones, a very pleasant woman. We rode through Hamilton Co.

Dec 4th Made about twenty seven miles through Ray Co, and put up for the night at a Mr. Roddie's place, that is, all but Frazier; he stopped farther back at another house.

Dec 5th We turned out at day light, and while we were washing up for breakfast here came F, trudging along on foot with his saddle, bridle and blanket on his back; looking the picture of forlorn troubles, I asked him in a sympathizing tone, "Whats the trouble, and where is your steed." "I shust found dot horse gone and tied." So poor old raw bones had given up the ghost during the night. His mule gone, his horse dead, after breakfast, we started again. F. hid his saddle in some bushes, but retained his bridle, and tramped on foot. After a few miles F. picked up a stray horse. He looked as though he had been turned out to die a natural death, was blind of one eye and string halted; however every thing is meat that comes to F's basket, so without trouble, he caught and bridled the animal, and mounted bare back except his blanket was strapped on him. F. was in high glee at his find; How that beast did churn the ground with his hind feet at every step, first one leg would be elevated as high as possible, and thumped down on the hard ground, then the other would follow suit, until F. was rattled and jarred all up and down his spinal column. "Poys vots der matter mit dis old cow, any how," he exclaimed, and then we roared again, at the comical picture. We rode about twenty-eight miles, F stood it like a major, considering his anatamy must have been in the last stages of dislocation. We passed Loudon which is to the right of our route and put up at Mr Hayes place in Roane Co.

Dec 6th Nothing occurred to disturb the monotony of our journey today, except we lost Frazier he not being able to keep up. Passed through Kingston, and put up at Mr Boyds place.

Dec 7th Arrive at Knoxville, but did not stop, passed on through the town, and crossing the Holston River, found our troops encamped and reported at HdQrs.

Dec 8th On duty with the General. Rode into Knoxville. Genl Granger joined the party, and we all rode out to Ft Saunders [Sanders],[1] to look over the ground where Longstreet's men made unsuccessful efforts to capture the fort. It is situated upon a rise of ground. The breast works are heavy, and a deep ditch surrounds them. All the trees in front had been cut down, the stumps left standing knee high. A net-work of telegraph wire stretched from

[1]The attack on Ft. Sanders (not Saunders) took place on November 29th. The fort was named in honor of Brigadier General William P. Sanders.

stump to stump. An attacking force would not notice this, until right upon it. The men in the fort reserved their fire until the enemy fell over the wires, which threw them into confusion. Then our men opened up with musket and cannon, poring in at short range, a most galling fire. This demoralized the enemy and they retreated back into a ravine, which sheltered them. Reforming their lines, they made another brave attempt, this time they jumped over the wires, and in the face of a deadly shower of shot and shell, reached the ditch, jumping into this, a shower of hand grenades was launched upon them, which must have played sad havac among them. But they kept on and attempted to climb through the embrasiors, through which the black muzzles of the cannon pointed, with these spaces full of struggleing humanity the guns were fired, and the enemy shot all to pieces, and each space was cleared; this was too much for any one to endure. They gave up the struggle and departed, so ended the strife. Longstreet withdrew his men and circling the town, went through East Tenn into West Virginia. Counting his losses, at Chickamauga and here at Knoxville, the killed, wounded and prisoners, it is safe to estimate he is returning to Richmond with not more than half the force which he brought with him, and with a firm conviction that the western troops know how to fight.

Dec 11th Our H'dQrs move into town, Genl [John G.] Foster supersedes Burnsides, who is going East.

Dec 15th Our Division march to Blains Cross Roads at Strawberry plains and go into Camp.

Dec 25th I am called up at 11 o'clock P.M. and went over to Genl Sheridans tent for orders. He was in bed on his cot and wrote his dispatch without getting up. Told me to make all haste to the depot five miles away and see that the dispatch was sent over the wires at once. It being a chilly night, he invited me to have a drop to warm me up; I accepted, and mounted and went off at a gallop. Knowing about the right direction only, not having been there before, fortunately I found the place without trouble, left the dispatch with the operator, and he informed me I could save some two miles returning by taking a shorter cut through the woods. I took his advice and to my regret. There was a hazy moonlight which served well enough on the main road, but in the woods, it was dark. However I struck the trail or cow path, and swung along at a good gait. When through the woods I came to a strange road, which knocked me out of my reckoning, keeping on I came to a creek, and an old mill, with a house attached. It was about 1 A.M. but I roused up the house, and enquired my way; I got it with a growl from the man, for being disturbed at this unearthly hour for which I did not blame him; I was two miles out of my way, so the short cut proved a long one. I reached camp just before day.

Dec 31st At midnight a blizzard came on, and we shivered under our blankets until morning, when the storm abated, the sun came clear and bright again.

Jany 1st, 1864 New Years day. Our mess regale themselves on stewed chicken for dinner, barring the fact they were foraged by some of the boys, we relished the dish hugely.

Jany 2d The Genl. requested me to execute a mission for him, to go to Mrs. Nancie's Plantation, some miles from camp, and across the Holston River, and incidently present her with a canteen of fine, spirits-fermenti. I started early, and riding up the left bank of the river until reaching the point where I was to cross. Owing to recent rains, the river was raging high in its banks, and swiftly running. Reaching an old blacksmiths forge, with a log house attached; dwelling within this palace of logs, I found an old man of sickly hue, a young man with a cough and consumptive appearance, an old lady and two grown girls about 16 & 18 respectively. I asked the old fellow if he would put me over the river. He answered yes, and told the two girls to ferry me over. I was a little non plused at this, but concluded they must be used to the business, as they seemed to include in their slim persons about all the good health the family possessed. They shouldered their double end paddles, while I tied my horse to a tree near by, and led me down to the water; here was a dug out canoe, made from a single log. Of course it was perfectly round on the bottom and would roll over at the slightest inclination. It was a doubtful concern, and my hair does not part in the middle, in view of the fact, the river was a third of a mile wide in its present condition and on the rampage as well; the out look was dubious. I got in however very carefully, and sat on the bow; the girls got into their places, with such apparent confidence, that I thought they could either swim, or were old veterans at the business. I offered to do some of the paddling myself, but they said I had better set still, which I did with a good deal of mental activity. They managed the clumsy affair with neatness and dispatch, that would put to shame a Modoc Indian, and landed me in good shape, telling me to hollo over for them when I returned. I found Mrs. N's place without difficulty, and delivered my message together with the spirits. She insisted on my having dinner with them, as it was just on the table; I was not at all backward in coming forward, with thanks I accepted, and did full justice to the spread. After dinner I was charged with many polite messages to the General and returned to the river. My ferrymen or more properly speaking ferry women, were on the look out for my return, and came over, returning me to their side of the water safely. I paid them for their services in Uncle Sam's currency, and returned to camp.

Jany 7th During the night some thief or thieves stole two of our horses, Mine and Lakey's. This is the second theft in our camp. On the night of the blizzard Dec 31st There was a fine double white blanket stolen from each of the Genl's three horses. We hunted through the camp for our stock, without discovering any trace of them, So our Quartermaster was ordered to replace them with others.

Jany 14th Nearly all of the 51st have veteranized, and as I had made up my mind to see the war through to its termination, I rode over to sign the rolls; Lakey accompanied me and re-enlisted in his regiment. The roll is dated Dec 24th. Each veteran is to receive a thirty days furlough.

Jany 15th The Div. broke camp and started for New Market; all those who re-enlisted, march over land for Chattanooga. The Genl kindly gave me transportation by rail and boat. Accompanied by Marion, Phelps and two other HdQr boys, we walk to Strawberry plains Station, on the 16th there to await the arrival of a train bound for Knoxville. There being no regular schedule time, upon which the trains operate, the time is uncertain and we take quarters in a house with the provost guards.

17th We are up with the sun, and go down to the depot, only to learn there will be no train today. Disappointment perched upon our banner, and we returned to our temporary quarters. The day is spent in such time-killing, as our limited resources permit. We go to our bunks at 9 P.M. I had just got into the borders of the land of nod, when two of the guards, Jack Boston and Charley Allen started a row, which soon assumed the proportions of a prize fight, Sans any rules that are supposed to govern the London prize ring. The Sergt of the guards, hearing the racket came in; not being able to pacify them, he placed them both under arrest and marshalled them below to the guard room and left them to cool off at their leisure, and we slept in peace.

18th A train has come in, and at 2 P.M. we start for Loudon; passing through Knoxville. Reach L, after dark, disembarking, we tramp around in the mud and Egyptian darkness; finding an unoccupied shanty, we take possession, and start a fire in the fire place, basking in its cheerful influence, we take a snack from our haversacks, then spreading our blankets, turn in.

20th Spent a day here waiting for a boat, some natives brought in some *heavy*-light bread and corndodgers which we bought; the boat came up and after discharging its freight, we started down the river. At night fall the boat was tied up to await day light as the pilot was not familiar with the channel.

21st After an all day's sail we land in Chattanooga, and hunting up our old HdQrs, take possession, to await the arrival of our respective regiments.

24th The troops arrived, but must await the advent of the mustering officer, who is engaged elswhere; we are taking time easily, with plenty of grub, and are not worrying.

29th I conclude to explore the summit of look out mountain, procuring a mule of a very diminutive pattern, but having a record as a climber, I set out with my toes nearly scraping the ground. As small as he is, I find his staying qualities surprise his proportions, and would do honor to a much larger specimin of his ilk—climbing to the top of the mountain with all ease. Here I find a cluster of clean looking houses, in a village called Summerville. The place is being used as hospitals. Owing to the high altitude, the air is clear and bracing, which is greatly to the benefit of the invalids. Turning northward, I ride to the extreme point; there is a huge flat rock which projects over the point, which caps or roofs the straight face of a perpendicular ledge. Dismounting from my mule, as it were, I sit upon the extreme edge of the rock; my feet swinging in mid air, I prepared to enjoy the scene. An unobstructed view, north, east and west, a panoramic view is spread out before my sight, such as no canvas can depict, and is well worth a days journey to see. Lying nearly North is Chattanooga, quite three miles, as the crow flies, but it seems only half that distance, owing to the clear atmosphere. The Tennessee River running partly around the town, circling due south, it comes to the foot of the mountain then gracefully bends due west in many curves, playing hide and seek, in and out, among the woods, until it dwindles into a silver thread, losing itself in the blue distant haze. Directly below me in the river is an island, rising sugar loaf shaped, from the water, and so near under the brow of the mountain that it is over-shadowed by it. This is called Moccasin Point; upon its crown was placed a battery to assist

Hooker in his attack upon the mountain. Beyond this point and North of the river for twenty five miles or more, Anderson's Ridge is in view as far as the eye can reach until the misty green merges into the misty blue of the Heavens. To the right lies the Chattanooga Valley, spreading out in undulating waves of green, with a creek dividing its broad fields. This ideal picture is bordered or framed in on the south, by the irregular line of Mission Ridge extending eastward until it meets the curve of the river. The Ridge so recently bristling with all the destructive implements of war and which witnessed the sanguinary conflict, ending in a great victory for us and confusion to the enemy. A few steps from where I sit, stands the earth works within which were planted the two long siege guns, old long Toms, which sent their big shells into our camp, and town, and which done comparatively little harm as compared with their destructive powers, when properly handled. In the now peaceful valley, carpeted with green and yellow, I can see Fort Granger, which rising like an island from the surrounding fields, and where in stood Genl's Grant and Granger watching the assault upon Mission Ridge, overlooking the boys in blue, while they carried out to a successful issue the well laid plans of the Commander in Chief. It is said that from this point of the mountain, on a clear day and with a good glass, one can view the land within the borders of five states, to wit: the southern boundry of West Va. and North Carolina; eastwardly, across the northern boundry of Georgia, standing above Tennessee and looking westward into Alabama. After enjoying the beautiful scene, to my hearts content, and again, mounted my little mule, we made our way back to camp. I was well satisfied with my trip.

Feb 8th The regiment having been placed in line, we were duly mustered into the service for a second term of three years or during the war, as veterans. And are ready to receive the furlough promised us.

12th By a special train we left Chattanooga, passing through Nashville, and disembark at Louisville Ky. and are quartered at the Soldiers Home. A party of us getting leave went down town and visited Woods Theatre; witnessed the play "Mazeppa". It did not interest me much, except the principal part, where a real horse, a firey untamed steed, as it were, was led prancing upon the stage. The Prince was tied upon his back with his head hanging over behind. The animal being released, rushed up an encline representing a mountain, passing out of sight and shortly after, he staggered in from the flys, and fell apparently exhausted, and gave up the ghost most naturally, while the Prince was released almost dead after his wild race.

15th Passed through Indianapolis, reaching Chicago on the 16th, Going into quarters at the Soldiers Rest. Here we receive our back pay and furlough for thirty days, and are turned loose to shift for ourselves.

Feby 19th My Brother and I conclude to visit our old home town Kankakee. We stand not upon the order of our going, but go at once; on our arival we are welcomed with open arms by our old friends, who forthwith inaugurate social gatherings, and evening parties in honor of our return. That we enjoyed all this, goes without saying. We remain until Mch 4th, when we return to Chicago each one hundred dollars richer. Kankakee County paying this bounty for all re-enlistments, we conclude to go East, to Providence, R.I., the place of our nativity. Securing our tickets via the P Ft W & C R R. we land in N.Y. on the 7th, Hungry as hunters; getting a lunch we take a stroll up Broadway, visit Barnums Museum, and go to the theatre in the evening.

Mch 8th Spend the day seeing the sights of N.Y. and about 5 P.M. go to the north pier. Take a Sound Steamer for Groton on the Stoneington Line.

9th At early dawn, reach G. and transfer to a train which in due time lands us at our destination, Providence. We go at once to Sister Marys home, and are heartily welcomed. As soon as we were fairly settled She forth with set to planing ways and means to make our short visit as pleasant as possible. She having a large circle of friends and acquaintances, the plan of campaign was soon inaugurated, subject to such changes as circumstances should determine.

18th The past ten days, have slipped away with such rapidity that we can hardly realize that it is time for us to depart. What with the social evening gatherings, with Music and impromptu dances, a party on the shores of Narragansett bay, together with a clam bake of "ye olden time," boating, bathing, and sailing upon the broad bosom of the beautiful bay, Taking all together, it has been a most pleasurable time for "we exiles," a period we shall long remember, and con over its details when we are again at the front, at the seat of war. Molly, Cal and I make our rounds among our friends, bidding them good by, and take our departure, turning our faces again westward.

20th Reaching N.Y. we continue on through without stopping, cross over to Jersey City and take the Erie Road. Upon reaching Buffalo we conclude to stay a day, it being Sunday. After breakfast we take a stroll, go down to the docks, and view the shipping on Lake Erie, where-on was fought the great naval battle by Com. Perry in the early years, when the Republic struggled to perpetuate its liberties.

21st Took train on L S & M I Road for Chicago, arriving in due time, and in good order.

27th The past five days, we have visited our many friends, and acquantances enjoying our selves merrily. At 5 P.M. we are again on the cars, on our way South. Settling into my seat as comfortably as circumstances will permit I fall to thinking over our experiences of the past month. Regretting that it is all over, that the time has passed so swiftly away, yet it seems long, so much has been crowded into the few fleeting days. The clack; clack; of the swiftly revolving wheels, as they pass over the joints of the rails, makes a sort of a rythmical music, lulling to ones senses. With closed eyes, my mental vision pictures the various scenes through which we have passed. Turning to the future also and wondering if we may again return to these scenes, when the war is done. If we may be among the lucky ones that shall pass safely through the dangers, and trials that await us, when we are again facing the enemy. This short term of pleasures, sandwiched in between the two years passed and the years before us, will long dwell in our memories, and help to lighten the many tedious hours, in camp and field, in the land of tribulations and trouble, down South.

31st Mch We reach Nashville Tenn. and find nearly all of the 51st had reported, and were quartered in the Zollicoffer building, awaiting the return of a few laggards, when they would start for the front. Orders came for the regiment to move at once; I bid Cal good by, and the rest of the boys in the Co. as they march off to the depot. I being on detached service, remain.

Chapter VII

Wherein Smith, returning from his furlough, catches up with the headquarters of his division at Loudon, Tennessee. In March Grant has been promoted general in chief of all the Union armies and is now in the East; in April, Grant brings Sheridan east to head the cavalry of the Army of the Potomac. Brigadier General George D. Wagner now commands Smith's division, but he is soon succeeded by Brigadier General John Newton. Sherman is now in overall command of the Military Division of the Mississippi, with Thomas leading the Army of the Cumberland, McPherson the Army of the Tennessee, and Schofield the Army of the Ohio; Sherman's objectives are the Confederate forces of General Joseph E. Johnston and the city of Atlanta. General Johnston, who has succeeded Bragg after the Chattanooga battles, will oppose Sherman with both the Army of Tennessee, which consists of two corps (commanded by Hardee and Hood) and the Army of Mississippi (commanded by Polk).

Smith becomes General Newton's orderly and moves with his division—the 2nd of the 4th Corps—toward Atlanta through the actions of Tunnel Hill, Buzzard's Roost, Dalton, Resaca, Kingston, and New Hope Church. The campaign is basically one

*of maneuver through the rough Georgia terrain,
Sherman outflanking rather than making frontal
attacks, Johnston biding his time, waiting for Sherman to make a mistake. The maneuvering continues, and Smith marches through Acworth and to
Kenesaw Mountain, where he sees General Charles
G. Harker killed in action; the frontal assault on
Kenesaw is an unhappy failure, but Sherman, by
maneuver, again forces Johnston to retreat. Smith
finds a free dinner in Marietta and there fixes an
ailing clock.*

April 7th Securing my transportation papers, I
start for Chattanooga; arriving in due time, learn
that Head Qrs is established at Loudon. Boarding
an out going train on East Tenn RR. Reach L, and
camp, report for duty. The boys welcome me back,
from my brief experience of civil life. I find some
changes have occurred since I left them. Grant has
gone to Washington, And our Genl Sheridan has
also gone to the Eastern army and placed in command of a larger force than his old division, where
his ability will have a larger scope. He is a man, and
commander whom all respect, that come in personal
contact with him; we all felt that he deserved a
much broader field to display his higher ability. It
remained for Grant to find this out. Brig Genl
[George D.] Wagner of the 1st brigade is in charge
of our division.

18th Orders to move to Cleveland Tenn. Tents are struck, the camp broken up, and the line of march taken up. Passing through Sweet water, Philadelphia and Athens; cross the Highwasa [Hiawassee] River and go into camp on the 21st.

Preparations are on foot for an extended campaign. All needed supplies are coming in daily, such as ammunition, large and small; Hard tack, sowbelly, beans and coffee for the inner man, corn, oats, and hay, for the beasts of burden. Genl Wm T Sherman is commander in chief; Genl G H Thomas, "Pap" Thomas the reliable, as we call him is commander of the Army of the Cumberland.

May 3d At day break, the whole army is astir getting breakfast, after which, tents are struck, and all movables packed in the wagon train. The long roll is sounded, the bugles sound their shrill music, the lines are formed, forward, march, and the campaign is opened. On to Atlanta is the word.

After the long rest the army have enjoyed, with the rank and file strengthened, the army comprised of soldiers, who have experienced many campaigns, fought many battles, with experienced officers, tried and able commanders. The army starts out with every confidence in themselves, confidence in their officers and above all, confidence in the just cause which brought them here. These two splendid Armies, under Sherman and Thomas, with corps commanders, Joe Hooker, [James B.] McPherson, [John A.] Logan and Howard (the one armed preacher),

Atlanta Campaign

Genl. Smith A [ndrew] J. and others, equally brave, and able, one may believe that this may be the beginning of the end of this great struggle, that we may sweep this whole western country from the Tenn. river to the Gulf of Mexico, free of all hostile enemys, leaving no foot of soil for them to camp upon.

Many are the perils we must encounter, many skirmishes, and battles must be fought and victories won; many hundreds, perhaps thousands of good and true men, may fall, and find a grave by the way side. This splendid army, nine tenths of whom are veterans, must go on to victory.

4th Genl Wagner is relieved, and returns to his brigade, Genl [John] Newton (Maj Genl Vols.) assumes command of the division. He is an F. F. V. and west pointer. He has done me the honor, to appoint me as personal orderly, which prospectively keeps me in the saddle when he is mounted. We ride to Genl O O Howards HdQurs. (our Corps Commander), and we all go to Catoosa Springs, Ga. This was a famous health resort before the war, a sort of Saratoga in the South (barring the lake). But the place is supplied with numerous springs, some twenty seven of them, and what is most remarkable, each one flows a different water, and christened accordingly. The original sponcers must have searched deeply the medico encyclopedia. Here is a few of them, Charlybate, Buffalo, Emetic, Choutnabosqua, Red-Black-Blue and White Sulphur, Healing, Bedford, Coffee, Epsom and Congress. I must not forget to mention the Sand Stone, the only one among the lot, that is pure and tasteless. And after we had tested a dozen or so, each worse than the other, we had to fumigate our systems, as it were, by drinking freely of the latter. The Black Sulphur is the nastiest of the lot; one would suppose the water must flow through a whole cartload of ancient eggs. If there be any virtue in the great variety of these waters, and their healing qualities equel their numerosity, then indeed here is a spot on earth, a mecca for all the ills man is heir to. The large brick buildings must have been Hotels, but in their present delapidated condition, they are only fit to house familiar ghosts.

7th A sharp skirmish took place at Tunnel Hill. The enemy was promptly out flanked, and retreated.

8th The Genl ordered our Capt. and fifteen of us escort to reconoiter an old road; we had not advanced far, when we ran against a rebel skirmish line, exchanging a few shots with them to develope their strength, returned to HdQrs and reported the situation.

9th Our advance found the enemy well posted on Rocky face Ridge, and Buzzards Roost. The 3d Brigade ([Charles G.] Harkers) became engaged sharply. The place is well named, it being a rock ribbed ridge, with a few scattering trees. The top is covered with projecting rocks, from one to eight feet high, forming a natural protection for the enemy; our men scaled its side driving the rebs from piller to post

Sad Search for a Missing Soldier

with loss on both sides. Sitting on my horse on top
of the ridge I can look down into the valley to the
left, and see the 23d corps advancing against the
enemy there. Also have a good view of the enemys
position, while our 3d Brigade is well occupied, a
force of rebels are seen advancing below with a view
to flanking the ridge, and get a cross fire on us. Orders are sent to retreat slowly, far enough to prevent
this, which is done, while another force is sent to
out flank them, when the rebs fall back and retreat
southward.

13th Dalton evacuated, and is occupied by our
troops. Moss and I rode back to take a look at the
scene of the fight on the 9th. It is as wild a place as

it is possible to imagine the huge rocks sticking up on every side like pointed monuments in a grave yard. Our dead are still unburied, and lay where they had fallen, stripped of every vestige of clothing, their nude forms exposed to the hot blistering sun; one dead rebel lay near one of our own, who perhaps was fatally wounded but with life enough to shoot this robber of the dead, while he was engaged in his nefarious work. It is the usual practice of the enemy to strip our dead, when they fall into their hands; I suppose they think, to the victor belong the spoils.

15th Advancing near Resaca, find the enemy strongly intrenched. The 3d brigade made a charge driving the enemy back into their trenches, and form in line with the rest of the division; a line of breastworks is being thrown up. The 51st being in the charge, I ride over to see if Calvin is all right. [Robert F.] Crawford said the last he saw of him he fell while they were advancing double quick. With much anxiety I rode back over the field, and searched among the dead and wounded, but found no trace of him. It was now growing dark, and I went back to the regiment, and was greatly relieved to find he had turned up all right. He said that while running, his foot caught in a root and he floped over in great shape, just as they right obliqued; when he caught up to the line, he found himself with another regiment, and after the charge ended, he hunted up his company.

This afternoon, while a Pennsylvania battery was firing shells at the enemy's works, three officers were observed riding up to the rear, of them, sitting on their horses, they examined our position through a field glass, one of our gunners sighted his steel gun at them and fired, knocking the middle one from his horse.

16th A force was sent to out flank the enemy's position. They quickly abandon their works, we quickly follow them up and crowded them so closely they could not destroy the bridge, which spans the river. So we are enabled to use it.

18th Skirmishing is the order of the day, steadily advancing, the rebs retreating. If they attempt to make a stand, we speedily flank them, and force their retreat. And so it goes on, we give them no rest. Some prisoners falling into our hands say, "The officer killed by one of our batteries, is Lieut Genl [Leonidas] Polk." Passing through Kingston, we form camp about five miles south, for a short rest, and to enable our army to close up the gaps.

22d A number of men, who did not re-enlist in December, and whose three years time has expired, are sent to the rear, and will go home, pleased no doubt that they will see their people once more, after seeing so much of the war. Many of them no doubt will come marching back again, after a short period at home, accepting the big sums that drafted men are willing to pay for substitutes.

23d Promptly at noon, camp is broken up, and the army moves forward again, crossing the Etowah

river. We pass the smoking ruins of an old powder
mill, which has been used to manufacture that article for the Confederacy. Continue on far into the
night before coming to a halt.

May 25th Genl Hookers corps in front today,
heavy skirmishing near New Hope Church. It has
been drizzling fine rain all day. Our movements
have been so rapid, our teams are far in the rear, so
we have not tents to shelter us from the elements. I
have had little or no rest or sleep for the past forty
eight hours, and my horse is about done up. Our
division go to the front which we reach about 9 P.M.
and relieve one of Hookers divs. who retire to the
rear. The troops set to work digging trenches, and
throw up breastworks. They work like beavers, relieving each other. Soon after our arrival, our corps
commander Genl Howard borrowed my services of
Newton, his staff being all engaged. He sent me to
hunt up Genl Stanleys division, and lead them to
the place alloted them on the line.

It is so dark I can not distinguish one man from
another, three feet away. I only know they are some
where on the road coming up; riding back over the
ground Hookers troops had fought over, I encountered many a dead soldier. I could not see them
for the pitchy darkness, but my horse when he
came to one would shy and go round them; he
could either see or smell them, but would not step
over them. The road was filled with troops coming
to the front; by continual enquiry, as to what div.

they belonged to, I soon found Genl Stanley at the head of his troops. I made myself known to him, and delivered my order, a verbal one, and directed him where to form his line, in conjunction with our division. I then rode back to Genl Howard, who thanked me, and I returned to our Hd Qrs which was just in the rear of our works. I was ready to drop off my horse, for the want of sleep; my poor horse was as badly off, I gave him a good rubbing down, hitched him to a tree, and took a look around for a place to dump my weary bones. Morse and I found a couple of logs. We roll them just far enough apart to admit of our lying between them, using our saddles for a pillow, the logs were placed broad side to the enemy. Wrapping our blankets around us we embraced the bosom of mother earth, with a sigh of satisfaction. Just as we were falling into the land of nod, the ball opened. The lay of the ground was such, that there was a gradual rise from the breast-works to where we lay, so that we were as high as the top of the works, though fifty yards in their rear; any bullets that just grazed them would hit the ground we lay on. The front log was about as thick as our bodies. About the time we had settled down, one of our pickets posted only a short distance in front of our works, thought he saw something sus-picious moving in front of his vision, and fired his gun off at it; a dozen shots followed. The rebels thinking a night attack was on foot opened fire from behind their works all along our front, not five hundred yards distant from our line. The way their shot and shell came tearing over was a caution, our men thinking the rebs were coming, opened fire from the batteries, and the infantry pored in their lead; all the rattle of ten thousand rifles and fifty cannon, made a pandemonium of sound and awoke the echoes of the more than Egyptian darkness. All the boys ran down to get behind the works, yelling to Morse and I to hurry up. But we just lowered our heads from off the saddles and lay still, by mutual agreement; Mitchell commenced to utter a long string of curses, as he usually does when excited, but we paid no heed to him, we concluded we were as safe there as any where. We could hear the bullets sing over us, and now and then "zip" one would bury it self in our logs, or glance over its top; the shells all passed over too high to hit anything but the trees, or sail through their branches.

For the thirty minutes it lasted the air was pretty well filled with flying lead and iron. It finally dawned upon the enemy, and our men, that there was not going to be any assault from either side; firing ceased, almost as suddenly as it had commenced, when quiet reigned again. The contrast, of the stillness was so great, from the thunderous roar, that one could almost hear a pin drop, but the air seemed to quiver or vibrate, or the drums of our ears caused the feeling. The boys all returned to their evacuated positions, and finding us all safe, turning in I went to sleep in no time.

May 26th It is learned, the cause of the racket last night, came about in this wise: our picket lines were stationed while the works were being thrown up; just beyond them, when our works were finished the pickets were advanced, and in the Egyptian darkness, they came in contact with the enemys pickets. The mutual discovery caused one of our men to fire, he supposing an attack was contemplated.

The other pickets followed suit, and thus the battle was opened; our picket line laid down and escaped the showers of lead and iron that came from our works and the enemy's, and escaped total destruction. The near position of the rebel works was discovered by the flash of their guns, so when the air battle was done, our pickets fell back nearer our works, as did the rebels to theirs.

June 5th We are still holding our position, and some exciting event transpires now and then, owing to the short distance intervening between our lines and the enemy's. The rising ground to our rear makes it an exposed position, while most of the men hug the works for protection, some are careless, and walk around there. The rebs take advantage of this, and open fire at unexpected times, and every now and then one is killed or wounded. One poor fellow having received a letter from home, strolled back to the rear and sat down by a tree, large enough to protect him if he had placed him self back of it, but instead, he was foolish enough to sit in front of it facing the enemy. While engaged in reading, some reb sent a messenger of death into him, so the poor man never finished his letter. This morning, when day light broke, it was discovered the enemy had flown during the night, their works were empty.

June 6th Camp is broken up, and we march to Acworth and camp. A heavy rain is poring down upon us, as though we had not been treated almost continually with moisture too numerous to mention. Old Sol seems backward about coming forward from behind his bank of clouds; its very depressing to the mind, and extremely uncomfortable to the human body.

June 15th Since my last entry of the 6th each day has been marked by stirring events, almost continuous marches, and shifting positions. Daily skirmishes occur, with more or less loss in killed or wounded. We are steadily pushing the enemy back from pillow to post; while our line of communications is being gradually lengthened, that of the enemy is shortening up, as they near their base of supplies, Atlanta.

There are a couple of men belonging to our escort, who seem to have a mutual understanding. They noticeably avoid every danger. This has become so pronounced that the rest of us have discovered their game; when the bullets are flying, they are conspicuous by their absence. They are notorious of boasting, of their hair-breadth escapes, before they joined the escort, so the rest of the boys never let slip an opportunity to nag them, chaffing them without stint, especially old man Mitchell, who is not afraid of old nick himself. He gives it to them right and left, to the amusement of the rest of us. They never wink a wink, but go off and flock together, when it gets too hot for them.

June 19th Several of us, saddle up, and accompany the Genl upon a tour of inspection along the works. Two of the staff officers are with us, riding along in plain view of the enemy, who take the opportunity to train one of their guns on us, and send a shell into us, as we were bunched together; the gun was well aimed. The shell came along with its usual infernal shriek, and landed square on the side of one of our escort horses, just behind the riders right leg and passed diagonally through the animal, and out just in front of his left leg, striking the bones of the horses shoulder, exploded, sending fragments of the iron in all directions. The horse was dead in an instant, but strange to say, none of us got a scratch. The horses nearest were staggered, and Genl Newtons fat old yellow "cob" came very near tumbling over.

June 22 The Genl and I ride out among the pickets; I have to keep an eye on him, when he starts upon these trips, as he is prone to fall into the deepest kind of a brown study, when mounted upon his favorite "cob," whose gait is well calculated to put his rider to sleep. It is between a dog trot, and a side to side motion pace, as easy as a rocking chair. About the time I get ready to call his attention to the fact that he is out side our picket line, and may soon reach the enemys lines, some reb will send a bullet whizzing our way, and disturb his reveries and then being anxious about my own skin, I am pleased to see him wake up in time to return to our lines. Fortunately so far I havent had to suggest, that if he is going to attack the enemy he had better take some troops along; I expect I shall have to do it some time if he does not mend his ways.

26th The Genl sent me orders to saddle up, and accompany him. As he has selected me as personal orderly, I am in the saddle more frequently than the others of the escort. We meet Genls. Hooker Palmer, Howard, Gairy [John W. Geary] and Stanley, all major Generals. They ride to the front, and along the line of breastworks. The rebels spy us, and fire at us from their rifle pits; such a cluster of stars is seldom seen in such close proximity to the enemy. They all have two stars on each shoulder, except Newton, who never wears his, or very seldom; he leaves them hanging in his tent and wears an old army blouse, that together with a pair of kid gloves with the fingers worn off, down to the first joint, are his constant undress uniform. When a reb would poke up his head to take aim at us, some of our men in their rifle pits, would bob up and fire at him; some of the rebs must be quick aimers, for they had to take snap shots at us, then duck their heads, to avoid being shot by our men. Some of the bullets came uncomfortably close to us. The Genls. concluded that discretion was the better part of valor in this case; they concluded to retreat, to a safe distance.

27th The line of defences, in our present position, are facing Kenesaw Mountain, which is occupied by the enemy, behind the strongest line of defences, we have yet encountered. The lower line of works run along the base of the mountain, while the second or upper line, runs up and over the crown; our works were built at night, and are so close to the enemys, that neither side can advance a picket line during day light. But after night fall, the pickets are posted a short distance in front. This is the position of our corps front, which occupies about the center of the army. Orders came for a part of our division to attack the enemys works. The third brigade (Col Harkers) is selected. They form in line of battle behind the works. When all is ready, the signal is given, and they file out through a gap and form brigade front, under a galling fire from the enemys works. They charge at the double quick and in two moments, they reach the cheval-do-frise (a line of sharpened stakes driven into the ground at an angle of forty five degrees). These are removed under a close range fire, also a line of brush in front of the ditch; these are also sharpened and pointed outward. All this is quickly accomplished, while the enemy is pouring in a front and cross fire which is most destructive. With an opening cleared the ditch is crossed by one flag bearer who plants his standard upon the enemys works, only to receive a bayonet thrust, and he drops back leaving the flag within easy reach of the rebs, but every attempt on their part to snatch it, is frustrated, by a concentrated fire at every head that shows above the works. Then a handful of our men made a rush, and rescued the stars and stripes. The cross fire was terrible; a rebel bullet was liable to go through three men in line. It was a veritable death trap, like the famous charge of the six hundred at Balaclava in the Crimearean war. Our men were ordered to lie down to escape the deadly cross fire, continuing to load and fire in that position. Col Harker with only one orderly in attendance (he declined to take any of his staff), sat on his white horse, a fair mark for hundreds of rebel bullets. There he sat as immovable as a rock, while the bullets flew all around him. He must have known that nothing but a miracle could save his life, yet he never flinched; at last horse and rider fell together both mortally wounded. Several of the men nearest him, sprang up to carry him off the field; of these some were struck down at once, but others filled their places, to be in turn stricken down. With the assistance of the orderly, who had miraculously escaped being killed though his clothes were torn with bullets, they carried the brave officer back to our works. He was still alive, a surgeon took him in charge, and on examination, his wound was pronounced mortal; word was passed along the line of the men in front, and they all sprang up together and beat a retreat to our works. And now the curious fact is learned, that while our loss is heavy, it is not one half as much as we feared; most of our loss occurred while the men were charging, and pulling up the stakes; after they lay down, little damage was done, as the rebs laid their loaded guns on top of their works and fired without exposing their person. After night came on, those of our wounded, who were able, made their way back, and a searching party under cover of the friendly darkness, brought in those whom they found alive.

29th During a charge by the rebs, which was repulsed, a rebel captain got bewildered, and fell into our hands. Seeing no chance to escape he drew himself up to his full height, some five feet six or thereabouts, struck his expanded chest with his hand, and exclaimed, "I would rather be shot than surrender, a disgrace I can not tolerate." A sergeant stepped up to him, and said, as he placed the cold muzzle of his revolver in his face, "All right Captain, I will save your honor," The gallant captain turned white, when he looked down the black tube, and changed his mind instanter, and said "I surrender." His arms was taken from him, and he was sent back to the rear, with his head hanging.

The enemy have been flanked out of their strong position, and we are again pushing them back.

July 3d Not being on duty today, I rode out in front of our advancing column, and got in with the skirmish line, entering Marietta with them. The enemy retreating as we advance, exchanging shots; when they were clear of the town, I looked around, with a view to hunt up a dinner. I found a house with a vegatable garden in the rear, which looked promising; concluding to try my luck, I dismounted, and hitched my horse to the front fence, marched up to a fine looking old lady who stood on the porch, watching my proceedings. I politely made known my wants, at the same time, I told her I would act as guard to the premises while the army was passing through the town; no stragglers would be allowed to molest her. She looked me over with evident curiousity. No doubt she was wondering if I might be an average specimen of the yankee, of whom,—she had heard tell about—but had not seen any of them before. She replied, pleasantly she would get me a dinner, if I would wait for it to be cooked. Wait!! of course I would; she set about it at once. She did not display any anxiety, be cause of the retreat of the rebel army, and the yankees coming in; she seemed to be surprised that there was so little difference, between us and her own people. I did not question her as to what ideas she had harbored upon the subject, but I could see she had labored under the mistaken impression, that we of the North were of a different specie, of the human family. Many of the women in the south had some queer ideas about us, and even some of the men had formed queer ideas, as to our size, shape and manners, &c. The old lady was tall and spare, with abundant hair, which was as white as snow. She led me into the dining room to await the advent of dinner.

Glancing around the room I take in its details. What struck me most at first, was its great size, for a dining room for a private residence; large enough to accommodate several quadrille dancers; the table at which I sat, was long enough for a big boarding house, would seat fifteen or twenty persons. The floor, while scrupulously clean, was innocent of carpet except, an oblong rag mat such as mother used to make, laid in front of an old-fashioned fire place, which was broad and deep. A dozen primative chairs, with hickory strips interlaced for seats, giving them a decided home-spun look, a high mantelshelf over the fire place contained two or three tin candle sticks with half consumed candles stuck in them, a pair of snuffers of our Grand father's days, and last, but not least, an old, old clock, high and broad, with its veneered front, patches of the veneer missing, the lower part of the door with the usual daub, a landscape, with impossible trees, on the banks of a lake of very blue water, where it had not been scratched off, a veritable curiosity shop of old relics. The clock looked old enough to be gray headed, and was dumb as an oyster; not a single tick left in this time honored structure. Curiosity led me to examine the interior of the old machine. As my hostess was busy in the next room, with the door closed between, I opened the door of the clock, and gazed into its dusty depths. The dust of ages has accumulated within its interior; the works were made of wood, which precluded its age being at less than a century; the two iron weights rested upon the dust covered floor, as did the pendulum, where it had fallen, no knowing how long ago. I examined it and, discovered the trouble at once, and determined to fix it. If the old lady would kindly stay away a few moments longer, I would give her a surprise. The top of the pendulum, had broken off where it was flattened, and at the hole through which the pin goes that should hold it in position. With a fork I easily punch a new hole. With my knife blade I take the screws out, that fasten the square dial with its queer circle of pointed figures, slip the pendulum into place, putting a pin through, bending it down on each side, replace the dial, fish the key out of the dust; said key is not quite large enough for a well crank, wind up each weight carefully, for fear the cords might give way, turn the hand to the proper time, five minutes to two, start the pendulum swinging close the door, and resume my seat, and now the room echos with the solumn tick-tack, and the resurrection is complete. It goes along without hesitation, as though it was pleased to be in motion once more, and I imagine it is saying with its tick-tack, thanks-thanks. Chuckling over my successful Job, I just have time to draw a long face, as the kitchen door openes to admit my old lady, with her hands full of dishes. The tick-tack struck her at once, and

I thought she was going to spill all the dishes, in her shock of amasement; just then, the old wheels started to whirr, the sound resembled a saw mill in the distance, with a long wheeze, it finally struck one- two-. As solumn as an owl, I watched the old lady, as she set the dishes on the table, and walked over to the clock, and opened its door. Seeing the pendulum as it swung merrily to and fro, she heaved a deep sigh of relief and recovered, "Well I never, did you do that?" she exclaimed. "Yes-m" "Well I never, you must be handy," she remarked, as pleasant as a basket of chips, if I may be allowed the expression. She said it had not run, for more than a year and she had missed its noisy sound greatly, like an old friend gone from her; it was an old family relic, her father owned it before she was born. She bustled around and soon had my dinner spread before me, a nice one to, and I enjoyed it with a good deal of relish, and with a tranquil mind, as I had done a good deed. She seemed pleased at my appreciation of her cooking; when I had satisfied the inner man, having cleaned up most of the dishes set before me, I handed her a fifty cent piece, paper money, one of uncle Sams shin plasters. She hesitated about taking it, as I had doctored her clock, and there by had risen many degrees in her estimation of yankees in general, myself in particular. Bidding her good by, I mount my horse, and hunt up my division. I think the old lady will have a kindly remembrance for one yank, every time she winds up her venerable time piece.

Chapter VIII

Wherein Sherman's army continues toward Atlanta (with Smith still attached to division headquarters) and, after pausing to bring up supplies at Chattahoochee River, fights the Battle of Peach Tree Creek on July 20, which forces the Confederates into strongly fortified defense positions in the city. (On the 17th, Jefferson Davis, displeased with Johnston's delaying tactics, replaced him with the impetuous General John B. Hood, and it was Hood who started the Battle of Peach Tree Creek.) On the 22nd, Hardee vigorously attacks the forces of McPherson but is repulsed; General McPherson is killed in the fight, and with his death the Union loses one of its most promising officers. Sherman next moves to his right, and on the 28th General O. O. Howard, who has replaced McPherson, fights the battle of Ezra Church, southwest of the city. For a month, siege conditions prevail, and Smith does not enjoy the harassing Confederate artillery fire. Sherman keeps extending to his right (west and south of the city), cutting the railroads. The climax comes at Jonesboro, south of the city, on August 31, when Hardee attacks General Howard's troops but is repulsed. Hood begins the evacuation of Atlanta the next day while Hardee holds his positions at Lovejoy's Station to cover the evacuation. Sherman's troops enter Atlanta on the 2nd of September, leaving Hood entrenched at Lovejoy's Station.

Meanwhile, the Confederate cavalry leaders, Wheeler and Forrest, have been operating in Sherman's rear, and on the 24th Sherman orders one division to Rome, Georgia, and Smith's division to Chattanooga; five days later, concerned that Hood may move north, he sends Thomas to Nashville and General Morgan's division to Chattanooga. But Hood first moves west, to Palmetto, and then after conferring with Jefferson Davis begins to move north towards Tennessee, intending to cut Sherman's line of communication. If Sherman follows, Hood will look for an opportune moment to turn and attack; Sherman does follow but never quite catches Hood, finally abandoning the chase and returning to Atlanta. He re-inforces Thomas with the 4th and 23rd corps, plus cavalry, and gives Thomas the responsibility for handling Hood; on November 15 Sherman leaves Atlanta on his famous "March to the Sea."

Smith goes to Chattanooga with his division, is assigned to the adjutant general's office and sent for a few days to Nashville. He joins his division at Pulaski, Tennessee, close to the Tennessee-Alabama border, where he secures fresh meat through "moonlight requisition" and enjoys letters received from young ladies in response to a "personal" ad in the Chicago Tribune. But on November 22 Pulaski is evacuated to prevent its being cut off. The Union forces escape the trap Hood has planned for them and through a remarkable series of Confederate blunders escape again farther north at Spring Hill. At Franklin, the next town north, the Union forces dig in and repulse a Confederate frontal attack on November 30 in a battle that is remarkable for the frightfully high Confederate casualties. The Union troops then hastily withdraw and succeed in getting in behind the fortifications of Nashville. Smith is with the army all through this retreat and though General Wagner is replaced as division commander on December 2 by General Washington L. Elliot, Smith continues as an orderly with division headquarters.

July 5th Crowding the enemys flank and center, they are forced to retreat beyond the Chattahoochee River. They attempted to burn a large corn starch factory, but failed, in their haste to get away. It fell into our hand, together with an immense quantity of corn starch, ready for use. The Quarter Master took it in charge, and issued it out to the army in its immediate vicinity, and we enjoyed the luxury of

boiled corn starch pudding for supper. I accompany
Genl Newton to Genl Howards HdQrs. The boys
have dubbed Howard, the preacher Genl, as he
preaches some times on Sundays. He is said to be
strictly temperate, and swears not at all, an example
many of the other Genls might follow with profit.

July 9th Our division moved up the left bank of
the river to the vicinity of the late starch factory.
The ravages of war have visited it, and it has been
destroyed by order of some one, its blackened walls
a testimony of the ravages of war. It is said seven
hundred people, mostly girls some old women and
super numerated old men, found occupation here;
grim war has turned them out to the tender mercies
of a cold world. If the rebels had had time, they would
have anticipated the act and saved us the deed.

13th We are relieved by troops from the 13th
Corps, and cross the river at Howell's Ferry, camping
on the Atlanta road, about thirteen miles there from.
Wise acres and old women say the number 13 is unlucky. Here it is repeated three times: the 13th day
of the month, the 13th Corps relieves us, and we
camp 13 miles from Atlanta. The evil of it should be
inoperative, it being repeated in three incidents, or
is it cumulative? Who knows.

18th Army in motion again, our div. in front.
Reaching Nancys Creek, the rebel skirmishers dis-
pute every step of the way across the valley; on the
opposite hill we can see the enemys works. While I
was riding down the road which was filled with our

advancing div. I saw the rebs bring forward a cannon unlimber and place it in position to rake the road. They opened up with a six pounder shell, which came tearing along in a bee line down the center of the road, but passed twenty feet over our heads. I could see the shell as it left the mouth of the gun, and followed it with my eye, through its whole course. They had the range but not the proper elevation; our troops took the hint, and marched into the timber to the left. I rode forward, and took position a rod or two from the road, where I had a clear

Sherman's Headquarters near Atlanta

view of the rebel lines; some one of them took me for a target, and fired at me. Sitting perfectly still on my horse for if I moved, I might improve his aim, the ball came singing over, passing under my chin, tapping me upon the left shoulder; it was nearly spent, and struck the ground just beyond me. Getting off my horse, I tried to find it. Just then Col. [Emerson] Opdycke's horse was shot under him, just back of me on the road side. The Col. was unseated, and the horse killed; our troops out flanked the rebs and they retreated, leaving us a free passage across the valley and creek.

July 20th The third brigade of our div. in front as we get nearer to Atlanta day by day; the more frequent and stubborn are the skirmishes. Crossing Peach tree creek a line is formed on the rising ground beyond. As we were in plain view of a rebel line of works, and our right support has not yet come up, owing perhaps to the fact they had a more difficult route. The brigade commenced to dig a trench every other man having a spade. Genl [John B.] Hood seeing the unprotected condition of our right siezed the advantage without delay; quickly forming his men, he sent a force, who charged with the usual rebel yell. Our old third brigade were too old hands at this business, to give way; seizing their guns, they pored in volley after volley, thinning the rebel ranks. This at very short range, the enemy in their front gave way, but those that over lapped our right had only a line of skirmishers confronting them, and these were quickly eaten up. It looked pretty serious for our brigade, if their support did not show up quickly, with the rebel force a hundred yards in their rear right flank; just then a division of Hookers troops came up at the double quick, and not a moment too soon. They drove the rebels back with a rush leaving their dead and wounded behind. The rebels that made the charge at the brigade was led by Genl [Clement H.] Stevens[1] and he and his horse lay dead together within fifty feet of our line, with a lot of his men heaped up around him. This is the second time this Genl. has tried issues with our third brigade. He was in command of the forces at New madrid Mo, in sixty two; on his retreating from there, the third brigade under Genl Payne chased him for a half a day and well on into the night. Coming up with him our force divided, two regiments on each side of the woods in which he was camped, he surrendered before day light, with his five thousand men to our less than three thousand. And now at his second defeat, he has surrendered to a mightier foe then yankee hosts; death has claimed him for its own. During the fight, and while I was riding after Genl Wagner, a bullet struck me on the right hand, as it hung by my side; for-

---

[1]Smith persists in believing that Brigadier Clement H. Stevens commanded the Confederate troops at New Madrid, when Stevens was not even in Missouri at the time. General Stevens was wounded on July 20 at Peach Tree Creek but did not die until the 25th.

tunately my blouse hung in several folds loosely in front of my hand, and the ball was a glancing one, my fingers went to sleep for a while, but in the excitement I soon forgot it. We learn from some prisoners that Hood has just succeeded Johnson [Joseph E. Johnston]. If this is a specimen of his work, we may look for lively times before we reach Atlanta. Although Hood has a cork leg, he can fight like a veteran.

22 Genl McPhersons forces, moved up on the left of, and within two miles of Atlanta near the Augusta R R. The enemy met him with a large force, using a shallow cut in the R R. and all the houses in the vicinity for shelter, from which vantage ground they fought with desperation. After a hard contest, they were dislodged, and beat a retreat back into their defenses around the town; our loss was very heavy, and Genl McPherson, who was one of our most able Genls, was killed. His loss will be greatly felt both by the men under his immediate command, and the rest of our army. His death will be mourned by thousands, for his personal worth, and soldierly qualities.

In him our Commanding General will miss one of his ablest Lieutenants. Our division move up in line and throw up a strong line of works, overlooking the enemys defenses. We have now reached, and can see Atlanta, the objective point of this Campaign. The enemy with their full strength, are concentrated within the city. They are strongly fortified, and their works well manned with artillery, some of which are of heavy caliber—as we have already been introduced to some of their big shells.

25th Our army have settled down for a regular siege. And after nearly three months of marching, over some pretty rough country, the rest, is most welcome. It has been a campaign that will long be remembered by those engaged in it, the enemy leaving no stone unturned to retard our progress. Innumerable skirmishes, and many battles have been fought. They selected their ground, where ever nature could aid them, and only retreated, when in danger of being out flanked, or to prevent a general engagement; when we confronted them in their strongest position, at Kenesaw Mountain, it was said by them, that Sherman was afraid to make a direct attack upon them, always preferring to use his superior forces in flank movements. Whether this was true or not that they (the rebels) had made use of this taunt, in order to cause an attack to be made, or whether the attack was ordered for another purpose, is a question. The facts remain that we did make a fruitless effort upon them, in the strongest position they held during the whole of the campaign; true they evacuated, directly after, but this was the result not so much from our threatening front, as from our threatening their rear. The aggregate loss to both armies must be considerable. It is true that while the enemy could less afford their losses; it is also true perhaps, that many of our own losses might have been avoided, to some extent.

Over in Atlanta, they have planted one of their heaviest guns. It being on a slight elevation, we can see it without the aid of a glass; with out looks stationed on the top of a high building they signal to their gunner, how to point the gun, so as to do the most damage, aiming at the diferent groups of Head Quarter tents, with a view to sending some of our general officers to kingdom come. They had our headquarters dead to rights. While one of the boys and my self stood talking together, just as our darkey calls dinner, a big camp kettle from this gun came along, and passed a few feet above our heads, making the most infernal noise, as it cut the air. We felt the wind from its swift rush as it passed; turning our eyes, we saw it strike the side of a tree just below us, taking out a chunk half its size; exploding, it smashed the rear end of one of our wagons, and killed a mule, that was tied to it. It raised a smoke big enough to hide its work of destruction for a moment. We went to our dinner, where our darkey cook stood with his eyes as big as saucers, "golly but dat was a tight shave," he said, as soon as he recovered enough to talk. While we all stood around the board, bang went the old gun again, and pretty soon came another shell, directly in the path of the last, and although it seemed incredible, we saw it strike the self same tree, in the same groove its predecessor had made, making it only a trifle broader. We could hardly believe our eyes, and so went down, and examined the tree,

This Fifteen-incher Spoke Loud

sure enough the evidence was indisputable. The two shells had traversed exactly the same route varying only a few inches; the distance from the gun to the tree is not less than two miles.

They kept up their fire at intervals the rest of the day and all night; by bed time we had become so familiar with the noise, that we did not mind it. The infernal music of the shells, varied through a whole octave; if it was traveling very fast, it sounded in a high key; if it came more leisurely, we dubbed it a base note, and so the tune went on all night, from do-to ra- with sharps and flats now and then. We felt no apprehension when they played on the upper notes, as that indicated the shell would go far beyond our resting place, but the base notes might mean it was going to fall short of, or in among us.

At the works just in front of our division a battery of siege guns were placed. This after noon, while our gunners were working them, driving some of the longest rifled shells, over into the rebel works I walked over, and got on top of our works, and stood along side one of these long guns. Just beside the embrasure, about midway the gun, when the gun went off, I could catch the flight of the shell the instant it left the muzzle, and follow its whole course, see it strike, and explode, showing how quick is the human eye. When a puff of smoke from the rebel works, would indicate they had returned our fire, I could drop down behind our works before their shell could reach us.

July 26th to 3d Aug[2] At or just after midnight we were roused up from our *peaceful* slumbers, orders having come to leave the camp standing and march, strict orders to make the least noise possible. Moving some distance to the rear, we took a westerly course, and circled around Atlanta. The march was continued until Atlanta was left in our rear and we reached the vicinity of Lovejoy station, attacking the garrison there stationed, and soon cleaned it out. Meantime the rebs sent a force to investigate

[2] Here Smith is again off on his dates. The Ezra Church fight was on July 28 and the action at Jonesboro on August 31—not July 31. Atlanta fell during the night of September 1–2 when Hood pulled his troops out of the city and down to Lovejoy Station; Union troops entered the city beginning September 2nd. The entry beginning September 25th is accurate.

Wrecking Railroads Becomes Fine Art

Rail-Twisting Tool Used by Sherman's Army

the cause of our empty works, but soon discovered
where we had gone, made haste to pick up all their
movables, burning all else, to prevent them falling
into our hands. The 19th regulars had destroyed the
rail road south of Atlanta, so the rebs could not
move any cars, so they set fire to them, burning a
good deal of ammunition, shells &c.

Aug 8th Genl Slocums troops were the first to enter Atlanta, after the evacuation. At midnight we took up the line of march towards the late besieged city. A fearful rain storm came up, we all mounted, and sat in our saddles, with our rubber ponchos around us; we were surrounded by more than Egyptian darkness, while we waited for our place in the marching column, one of the staff broke out singing- Mary had a little lamb- with all the variations, and we all joined in the chorus, with the wet accompaniment of the falling rain as it pattered among the tree leaves above our heads. Marching until the morning light we passed through Atlanta, and went into camp on the Decatur R R. In the afternoon Perv, Lakey and myself rode into town, to take a survey of the city. The effects of our siege was manifest upon all sides. Many of the buildings were partly or wholly destroyed by our shells. The depot and some houses which the rebels burned, did not add to the beauty of the desolate place, the ravages of war illustrated.

Sept 25th The army has enjoyed a good long and much needed rest. Have had plenty to eat, and only exercised in the usual routine of camp duties. On Sundays, our preachers have held services, as usual, incident while quietly in camp. This is Sunday, and the weather is all one can desire.

The peace that reigns, is broken. An orderly from Corps HdQrs. rides up to the Genls tent, salutes the guard, who announces his arrival to the Genl—

entering with his dispatch. Now then whats up; we soon learn. Three of us orderlies, are called to boots and spurs, and we each ride with our orders to each brigade, and the quiet peacefullness gives place to bustle and preparation. Tents come down, camp is broken up in haste, as though the enemy were upon us. A long train of cars is in waiting, and we are soon on board bag and baggage; our horses occupy one of the cars, and we are soon sailing northward for Chattanooga. Thus it is ever in a soldiers life; one hour we are surrounded by peaceful comfort, the next finds us in uproar and action.

26th We arrive in Chattanooga in due time, the journey accomplished in a few hours, while four months was consumed campaigning over the same territory. The third brigade remained on the train, and continued on to Bridgeport, Ala.

Genl Newton is relieved as division commander and I hear he is ordered to Dry-Tor-Tugas,[3] among the Floridy Keys. Brig. Genl Wagner is in charge in his place.

Oct 12th I receive orders to report to the A. A. G. and am assigned to a desk in his office, and join the clerical force and mess.

Oct 27th Our official records and books, are stored at Nashville. The A A G requiring some of

---

[3]Smith makes it sound as if Major General John Newton was sent to the infamous Dry Tortugas Prison in disgrace, when in reality he was sent in October to command the District of Key West in the Department of the Gulf.

them, I am ordered to go for them, transportation papers are furnished, and a requisition, and a weeks leave of absence. I board the train for N.

29th Reach my destination, go to the Kossuth House, secure a room and get breakfast, after which, I call upon the Post Q.M. with the aide of his assistant in charge I secure from the warehouse our HeadQuarter boxes, which we dug out from the thousand and one belonging to the Army. Selecting the papers and books required, I boxed them up, and sent them by the next train. This duty accomplished, my time is now my own for a day or two, I conclude to take in the town. About the first person I met, was Moore, also a clerk in our office and who was up here on a short leave of absence. We joined issues, visiting Duffields theatre in the evening and witnessed the Flying Dutchman; a mystic ship sailed across the stage over a storm beaten sea, accompanied by thunder and lightning, quite a realistic scene. After the play I took Moore to my hotel, and we bunked together. Some time ago we had jointly gotten up a personal, which we sent to the Chicago Tribune, asking for correspondence from the young ladies in the North, from those who could sympathize with two lonesome soldier boys. I assumed the nom-de-plume- of Charlie Morton, while he was Harry Wilson.[4]

[4]The "Personal" advertisement which provoked these letters appeared in the *Chicago Tribune* on October 26, 1864, and read like this:
Wanted—Correspondence

30th Received a telegram from our Assistant Adjutant General to secure additional papers &c and return with them at once.

Nov 1st Not greatly pleased at the curtailment of my liberty, I get the required documents, and accompanied by Moore, we are enroute, as orders is orders, and we must obey our superiors.

2d We reach Chattanooga only to learn the Division had departed, having received hasty orders to go to Athens Ala. So we take a return train back to Nashville, according to the orders they left for me, and take the western branch for Pulaski Tenn, and there await the arrival of our troops which were coming over land. We put up at the Tenn House.

Nov 5th The Division arrive and go into camp in the outskirts of town. Our HdQrs are established in a large mansion, the family move into one wing, while we occupy the rest of the rooms. Our AAG's office settles in the library, it being the best lighted, and best suited for our purpose. The house is situated within a fenced enclosure of several acres, with fine open timber just beyond. A large planta-

Two young gentlemen, highly respectable, of good moral character, are desirous of opening correspondence with as many loyal ladies *as see* fit to respond to this, with a view to friendship and mutual improvement. Ladies, do you desire a friend, would you like to be a friend? If you can with truth answer yes, then write to us, and our correspondence and time will prove that we can appreciate a friend. Particular attention paid those containing photos. Address Harry Wilson or Charlie Morton, Headquarters 2d Div., — C., Chattanooga, Tenn.

tion belongs to the place, mostly turned out to grass and weeds. Private Sam Wheaton of the 88th Ill is detailed to cook for our mess, and is an excellent one; every thing edible that comes to his hand, is sure to be cooked to the kings taste.

9th J M Arnold our chief clerk, Stull and my self went to town, and did not return until the witching hour of midnight. The moon shown through a misty cloud bank, giving an uncertain light. As we arrived at the gate leading into the grounds by a side entrance, we discovered a fat calf brousing about among the furrows in the garden. An idea seemed to strike us all three at once; upon comparing notes, we found it unanimous, to wit- the last fresh meat we had, caused a discusion, as we were gathered about the festive board, as to the genealagy, and age of the animal from which it came. It was decided that the said animal was too thin to cast much of a shadow, and the butcher had to prop it up against the fence in order to knock him down in regular style, &c &c, all this passing through our minds as we looked upon his-calf ship with longing eyes. Shaking hands all round, we decided then and there, that his carcass should grace the walls of our cook house before the rising of another sun. The moon still hid her face behind the friendly clouds, every body in the house, in the land of dreams. In front of the house was the usual sentinel on his beat, but if he should by accident discover our fell purpose, we could bribe him to silence with a good slise of cutlets. Arnold planed our mode of attack; we entered the enclosure, and made a circuit around our victim, getting him into a far corner of the Fence. This was done so quietly and silently, that it would have done honor to a modoc indian, upon the trail of a white man. With convenient stone in hand we closed in on mr calf, who began to sniff trouble, and made a dive for liberty. Stull siezed him by the nose, and was almost upset, by the shock; the stone came down between the eyes of the infant bovine, and down he tumbled, a knife severed his jugular, and in a moment his career was ended. Three Jack knives, were put in opperation, and we soon had the carcass properly skinned, and dressed; kicking a hole in the soft soil, the hide, feet and head were buried. Then taking up the remains, we transported them to our kitchen, and hung them up, then re-tired to our cots, chuckling at the surprise in store for Sam and the boys in the morning; we swore to eternal secrecy, and were soon in the land of nod.

10th Promptly we answered the call to breakfast, and in silence enjoyed the look of suspicion that greeted us, as we gathered about the board, and our olfactories took in the flavor of the pyramid of juicy cutlets piled up on the tin plate, that graced the center of the table. Bantering remarks were freely tossed about as feelers, but not a ghost of a smile did we three crack; we could see that Sam was dying to know how it came about, but we never let on. After breakfast, Arnold suggested that Sam be delegated to present the family of the house with a quarter of the veal, intimating to them that it came from the commissary department, which he did, and they accepted it with thanks. If they ever suspected it was a part of their own property, we never heard about it, so our conscience was relieved.

13th Since the advent of that veal, Sam has regailed us with it through the whole gambet of possibilities in cooking, cutlets, roast veal, veal stew, &c winding up with veal hash.

News has reached us that Mr. Lincoln (honest old Abe), has been re-elected president, and there is great rejoicing by all the troops. I also get twelve letters in the mail, answers to my add in the Chicago Tribune. Their post marks would indicate that the paper must have a broad circulation; they range from Nebraska to Connecticut and from Minnesota to the Mason and Dickson [Dixon] line. I wade through all of them, and find some of them interesting, and some otherwise; some are long as the moral law, others short and modest as though the writer did not wish to be too familiar on short acquaintance, or no acquaintance at all. Selecting the most promising, I put in some time answering; Moore received a bunch also, and we read each others.

22d Nov Our peace and quiet is again disrupted, by order to move. We pack up all the office goods and chattels in our charge, and place them in the wagons. It is said Genl Hood with sixty five thousand men is trying to get on our flank, and between us and Nashville. Our Genl Thomas is too wide awake to admit of any thing of that nature. Hood may be, and undoubtedly is a good fighter, but when he knocks against the rock of Chicamauga (Pap Thomas) he will knock in vain. It is also reported that Hood has boasted, he and his army will eat their Christmas dinner in Nashville; lots of events may occur in the coming month to alter his opinions. We march to Lynnville and camp.

24th Two hours past midnight we are up and on the road again, continuing on through the silent night, and reach Columbia Tenn; today the rebel Cavalry attacked our wagon train. The raiders accomplished nothing, as our infantry came up in time and drove them off after a small engagement.

Learning that the 72d Ills is some where in these parts, Will Sutcliffe is a member of that regiment, one of my oldest and best friends, from the town of three K's. After the fight was concluded, I rode over to where he is located, and spent an hour with him. They are holding a line of works, expecting an attack; we sat down in the ditch and chatted over old times. He is looking well, and takes things as they come philosophically. When I got back to HdQrs I found the tents pitched.

27th Still marching northward, cross Duck river, and throw up a line of breastworks. The enemy is close in our rear; our rear guard has fought all day with their advance. Hoods Army out numbers ours and he knows the fact, and is pressing us closely;

so far our retreat has been a masterly one, and is directed by a wise head in whom our army have the greatest confidence.

29th We reach Spring Hill.[5] The enemy have a strong force of Cavalry and some infantry on our flank. Our wagon train is so numerous, in order to protect it, we are necessarily retarded in our movements. If Hood knew our situation just at this moment, and had his forces well in hand, I think he could bring on a general engagement if he chose, with what final results, no one could foretell. There are many Generals, if they were in Thomases place, would no doubt push forward for Nashville regardless of protecting our wagon train as a whole, knowing the enemy is too strong to risk a general engagement; knowing too the rebs have had as much experience, as the army of the Cumberland, having seen as much service as our own men. In an engagement today Genl Bradley late Col of the 51st was wounded severely.

30th Our army marched all night, in order to get into Franklin before the enemy reached there. Lying in a curve of the Harpeth river, whose banks are high and steep, with a bridge spaning the stream over which all our trains and forces must pass, it is necessary to make a stand here until the army has got safely over. A part of our forces fall in behind

[5] A good discussion of the Confederate difficulty at Spring Hills is William T. Crawford's "The Mystery of Spring Hill," *Civil War History*, Vol. I, No. 2 (June, 1955), pp. 101–126.

some earth works, about noon. The enemys Cavalry were on our flanks all night long, but did no serious damage, to our wagon trains; we kept a good force of infantry with them. Our troops are glad to take a rest behind these works, after their long and weary march; the main body of our troops have already crossed, and are well on their way to Nashville, which is only eighteen miles distant. By 4 P.M. all our wagons were inside our lines and crossing the bridge as fast as possible. Most of the artillery has gone also, just a few pieces here and there along the works. The infantry left to guard the works, are strung out in a pretty thin line in some places, with a brigade in reserve to reinforce any point that might need them.

Between four and five o'clock the enemy opened up a terrific fire from their batteries. The shot and shell tore up the ground about the works in great shape, and made big holes in the houses just back of the line. Our skirmish line out in front lay down, and our men lay close up to the works, knowing full well what to expect next: a charge by the enemy. My horse having been turned over to one of the staff, his having gone lame it left me on foot, waiting for our HdQr teams to cross in their turn. When the Canonade opened, the shells flew in all directions, and hastened the movements of the mule drivers; our batteries opened up. A division of the enemy came into view across the field, our skirmish line retreating, as they advance. Our gunners worked the few guns they had for all they were worth, sending their shells through the ranks of the advancing enemy, making big gaps, which would close up at once. They started on the double quick at once, with yells from thousands of throats; our infantry opened fire, all along the line. The approach to the bridge being some what higher than our works, I could see every movement the enemy made, until the smoke hid them. Their main attack was against our right, where we had only a single line of men, although our fire reached them from every part of our line while they were crossing the field. Where the 72d Ill was, the enemy came right over the works, capturing some of them. Our reserve came up and drove them out again. The rebel Genl who rode a white horse, came right up to the breastworks; he was brave but fool hardy, for with his horses fore feet planted against the works, he was shot and killed, both horse and rider was riddled with bullets. Hundreds of the rebels were killed in that desperate charge; the rest lay down in front of the works while our men held the trenches. When the sun went down, and the shades of night drew its dark mantle over the bloody field, the enemy retreated and our troops crossed the bridge and took up their line of march for Nashville, burning the bridge behind them. I got into one of our wagons and rode to town. Many of the 51st were killed and wounded, those too badly hurt to be moved were left in charge of our Surgeons, who are left behind to attend them.

Dec 1st Reach Nashville early this morning. Our division take position on right of center near the Granny White Pike. The past ten days have been marked by trials and tribulations, almost constantly on the march, with skirmishing daily, all culminating in the fierce and bloody battle at Franklin last evening.

Dec 3d Genl [Washington L.] Elliott assumes command of our division; Capt J [esse] E Jacobs his brother-in-law is appointed A.A.G; Genl Wagner again returns to his brigade. Our HdQrs are established in a large house, belonging to a Mr Gordon. We clerks move our traps into the library, a large commodious room, containing a large collection of books, which I determine to investigate as soon as I have leisure time.

Our army is being rapidly placed upon a better footing, as to numbers, Supplies, ammunition &c. The fortifications, and forts are being strengthened on all sides; we have some heavy ordinance in the forts, and our field batteries are placed where they will do the most good.

Union Soldier's Candlestick

Chapter IX

Wherein Private Smith is in Nashville waiting for Thomas to burst out of the city and attack Hood. He is still with headquarters of the 2nd Division, commanded by Brigadier General Washington L. Elliott, one of three infantry divisions in the 4th Corps of Brigadier General Thomas J. Wood.

When the federal troops retire behind the well-developed defenses of Nashville, Hood does not have enough strength to attack, so he lays siege to the city. Thomas prepares a comprehensive plan for attacking Hood in what he hopes will be one of the decisive battles of the war. But before he attacks, he wants to equip his cavalry, now commanded by General James H. Wilson; he is, however, under the strongest possible pressure from Grant to attack immediately. But on December 8-9 freezing rain coats the ground and Thomas is unable to attack until the ice melts. Grant meanwhile prepares orders relieving Thomas and giving the command to Schofield, but the orders are never sent; Grant then orders General John A. Logan to take command but again changes his mind and starts for Nashville himself. The ice begins to melt on the 14th, and on the next day the attack begins (and Thomas is never relieved). Thomas first hits the Confederate right, but

the main attack is on the Confederate left as an en-
veloping movement. Hood is in serious trouble by
the end of the day, but does not retreat; on the 16th
Thomas repeats his attack, and the Confederates
are badly defeated; they begin their retreat that
evening, effectively pursued by Wilson's cavalry.
This is the end of Hood's army as a major and ef-
fective military force.

Smith visits a surgeon's tent the evening of the
first day of battle, and on the second day sees Thomas
deep in thought, seated on a log, his staff within call;
later he witnesses an attack by Negro troops. Smith's
division follows Hood, but when the Confederates
cross the Tennessee River, the pursuit is halted and
Smith goes to Huntsville, Alabama. Here Smith
attends a rural wedding, helps put out a fire in
headquarters, enjoys a reunion with his old friend
Morse, and applies for a furlough; he visits Nash-
ville, is ordered to Knoxville, Tennessee, and finally
arrives in Bull Gap, where his furlough orders
catch up with him. He reaches Chicago on April 8
and meets an old friend.

Dec 13th It seems, that the people at Washington
are getting restless, because Thomas does not pitch
into Hood at once. The wire pullers at our capitol,
are after his scalp. If Grant were in charge here, he
would politely, but forcibly tell them to—Go to—

he would open the fight when he was ripe and ready
and would not worry over their importunities. While
Thomas is next to Grant, in my humble opinion, as
a fighter, he is more modest and conscientious about
the destruction of his men. It is rumored that Thomas
is to be superceeded by Logan or some other General;
I do not think the army will take kindly to this if it
be true. No one can be held in higher esteem as a
Commander than our "Pap Thomas" is accorded by
the Army of the cumberland; they know his sterling
character, and have the greatest faith in his abilities.

Dec 14th The die is cast, ready or not, Thomas
must strike on the morrow. Orders are out that every
thing must be ready to attack in the morning; orders of instruction for each division and brigade
are being sent, and the rank and file are notified.
Many of the men set themselves down to write to
their homes in the north, some to their families,
some to their sweet hearts, knowing that perhaps
ere the setting of another sun, the hands that are
tracing the lines to some loved one, may be stilled
in death; no one knows who shall be taken, or who
shall be left. Hood has made his boasts, that he will
quarter his army within the city, and eat his Christmas dinner here. But he is counting his chickens
(or Turkeys) before they are hatched, as it were. In
case he makes his boast good, where oh? where will
the Army of the Cumberland eat theirs.

Dec 15th The friendly shades of night, has thrown
its dark mantle over us, covering both friend and

foe. Hoods Army are still beyond our outer walls, but the day has been marked by a most desperate battle, resulting in no especial advantage upon either side. Since early dawn, when the order was given to advance to the attack, after a tremendous bombardment of the enemys position, by all our batteries from forts and works, after tons of iron, shot and shell had been hurled into the enemys works, the infantry started forward. Ceaseless has the battle raged all day long; charges and repulses, with counter charges by the enemy, which were repulsed at each endeavor; encounters, between the works in open field each side charging the other in desperate action. Men have been slaughtered by hundreds, in some instances, the line officers of regiments have been all killed or disabled, leaving the non commissioned officer in command of companies. A large number of the enemys wounded are within our lines at this hour, but as the same ground has been fought over many times during the day, so many of our dead and wounded remain with the enemy. As darkness settled upon the field, the fighting gradually ceased, and as the army rested on their arms, the cooks came up, with great pails of steaming hot coffee, and cooked meat which each company receives. The reinforcement to the inner man, is much needed after the exhaustive struggle of the day. The ambulance corps are busily engaged, searching for the wounded, whether friend or foe. They are taken up, and conveyed to the surgeons tents; here they are laid upon a table, and examined, bullets are probed for, wounds stitched up and dressed, arms or legs cut off if too badly shattered to be saved. Indiscriminately, blue or gray, are attended to in turn as they are brought in; after the surgeon is done with them, they are sent to the general Hospital. Visiting one of these tents, used by our Hd Qr surgeon, I find him with his assistants, up to their elbows in gore; in one corner is a pile of members of the human system, arms and legs, hands and feet. A confederate is streached on the table, a long lank six footer, with a sponge held to his nose; he is unconscious that his right limb is being sawed off just below the knee. In ten minutes the limb is on the pile in the corner, the arteries taken up, the flaps of flesh are lapped over, and strips of adhesive plaster fastened over them, the bandages applied, and the thing is done with neatness and dispatch. In a few moments, he is revived, and holding up his stump, regards it with sorrow, and is carted away to make room for—next—who is a boy in blue, with a bullet through his arm, and one in his breast, and so the ghastly work goes on all night long. I turn in at a late hour, tired of seeing the victims under the surgeons knife.

Dec 16th While yet the sun lingers below his eastern hills, all is activity within our lines, while darkness still enshrouds the land. The cooks have brought forward and distributed hot coffee and cooked rations to the boys in front. All needed ammunition has been doled out, and as the first rays of the rising sun begins to streak the eastern sky, our batteries belch forth a rain of iron, at the enemy. The thunderous racket these engines of war create, as they send death and destruction into the enemys ranks, must be witnessed to be appreciated. The enemy open up their batteries in reply, as though bidding defiance to any attack. The air is filled with solid shot and shells, crossing each other, and it behoves one to lay low, for the hour it lasts; then a short lull. And now the real battle commences as our lines raise up and advance, upon the enemys lines. A large body of our forces become engaged, some parts of the enemys lines are penetrated, and many prisoners fall into our hands, officers and men. A determined charge by a force of the enemy, forces a portion of our line to give way. All the forenoon, the desperate struggle continues with some advantage to us as the rebels are forced into new lines. The rain of lead fills the air, and great numbers of wounded men are going, or being carried to the rear. As I am passing to the left of our division, I meet Genl Thomas, who is sitting upon the end of a log, his right elbow resting on his knee, with his hand nursing his stubby whiskers. He is alone, his staff standing by their horses within call in a slight depression below him, the bullets are kicking up the dust all around his vicinity; they seem not to be a disturbing element to his motionless figure.

It may be a fateful day with him, for today will decide for him; in success his promotion, in defeat, he is undone. The hissing of the bullets, nor the screech of the passing shells disturb him not; he is as motion less as the log upon which he sits. A fresh brigade of troops (negroes)[1] pass to the front. (Lieut Parks my old bunk mate before he was promoted) is in one of the regiments. They have not yet participated in the battle, but are now going in, charging with a yell that sounds above the rattle of musketry, and attracts the attention of the wavering rebels, who seeing the black faces of their foe, get into a frenzy, and fight like demons slaughtering the poor blacks fearfully. A brigade of rebels, came up to reinforce their decimated lines, and yelling, no quarter—to niggers, fiercely attacked them. And they had to give way, but brought some rebel prisoners back with them, and left behind a most unmerciful number of their dead. Poor Parks was shot all to pieces, among them. The rebels who were cap-

[1]There were two brigades of Negro troops in the Union army at the battle of Nashville. They were in a Provisional Detachment commanded by Major General James B. Steedman and constituted the 1st Colored Brigade commanded by Colonel Thomas J. Morgan (14th United States Colored Troops, 16th U.S.C.T., 17th U.S.C.T., 18th U.S.C.T. and 44th U.S.C.T.) and the 2nd Colored Brigade commanded by Colonel Charles R. Thompson (12th U.S.C.T., 13th U.S.C.T., 100th U.S.C.T., plus two batteries of artillery). Battery A, 2nd U.S.C. Light artillery was also in the battle. These troops were on the extreme Union left and made several determined attacks on Peach Orchard Hill, where they were repulsed with very heavy casualties.

Last Charge Brings Victory

tured by the colored troops, gave up with a very
bad grace; the officers especially, thinking it a disgrace to be captured by niggers, who, perhaps were
their former slaves, and whom may be, they had laid
the lash over their black backs before the war. One
rebel captain who was marching to the rear, siezed
the gun from the hands of one of his guards and shot
the negro down, but was promptly run through the
body by a sword in the hands of a white officer,
who was just behind him. Late in the after-noon our
forces make a concentrated effort, and vigorous
attack on all sides of the depleted ranks of the
enemy. A last charge with all our troops, and it is
successful, of most happy results. The discouraged
rebels throw down their arms by hundreds, or scat-

ter in every direction, except a few thousand who retreat in a body; the rest are routed, and the day is
ours. Hood with the remnant of his Army are in full
retreat. Most of their batteries, thousands of guns,
wagons, tents and supplies fall into our victorious
hands. The sun sets upon the sanguinary scene.
Misery, woe, and destruction upon all sides; every
part of the blood stained field holds its wounded
victims, and the dead, both blue and gray, inter-
mingled, everywhere. The field is filled with am-
bulances, and its corps of helpers, picking up the
wounded, black and white, blue and gray. The past
two days of mighty struggle, shows the courage and
endurance of our rebel foes, a courage worthy of a
better cause; and they were only whipped because
our troops were more determined to succeed, and
perhaps directed by a more masterly hand, than
Hood possessed. It seems that **Mr Hood** has changed
his mind, that the hospitality of his friends, among
the citizens of Nashville will be postponed indefi-
nitely.

Dec 17th Our division is on the road following
Hoods tracks. He is making for Mussel Shoals to
cross the Tenn. River. A storm of rain came up during last night, and it is still raining; the roads are
muddy, but the troops accept the mud with cheer-
fulness. Rebel stragglers are turning up singly and
in squads; they are hungry, foot-sore and weary,
and wet with the rain, and most thoroughly discouraged. Reaching the river, we learn that Hood

has crossed with not more than three thousand men; what a clear victory does this indicate. A few days ago, with a confident army of sixty five thousand men, which he is said to have had, reduced to this pitiful remnant; it means that it will be impossible to raise another army, in the west. With Hoods Army destroyed, the rebellion is crushed, or so much of it as relates to the west. Now let Grant and Sherman in the east, go and do likewise, and soon the banner of peace will wave over the again United Nation. We receive orders to march to Huntsville Ala. and go into camp.

Jany 5th The several divisions of the Army have settled down, each at its designated point, for the winter. Our Hd Qrs are located in a Plantation Mansion, about one and a half miles from H. The A. A. G's office as usual occupy the largest and best lighted room in the place; a Mr McCawley is the owner.

Jany 14th J M Baugher our fellow clerk has made a discovery. While we were enroute to our present quarters he fell in with a certain native; a little pumping on each side disclosed the fact that they were related. The said native's wife's cousin had an aunt by marriage, whose maiden name (before she married her first husband) was Baugher. They were delighted, especially the native. This forty second cousinship led to a confidential chat, in which the native said he had a daughter (Baugher beamed, and pulled up his collar); it got limp again at once, when he was told the young lady had a lover, and they were to be spliced on the evening of the 14th, today. John got an invite to the house, with permission to bring his friends, to witness the ceremony and dance with the bride, so we sleeked ourselves up, and after disposing of an early supper which our cook kindly hastened for us, we mounted our steeds, and started, fifteen strong, for the scene of action, ten miles away.

Baugher assumed command, none of our party being exactly certain of our route. After we had gone a few miles we made enquiry of a native whom we met. He said it was a right smart piece yet, but if u-ons want to take a short cut u-ons can go over the rise yonder, and turn off into the timber, and when you come to a clearing, turn to the left, and when you hit a road follow it to the place. Rather indefinite, but as we wished to arrive early, concluded to follow his advice. The sun had set and left a hazy moon light, which gave us an uncertain light through the trees; we found the clearing all right, but unfortunately took the wrong way out of it, got into a cow path, which we followed in indian file, and were landed up against a high rail fence surrounding a small enclosure in which stood a log house.

About seven dogs, of seven varieties greeted our approach with a combination of howls and yelps, which brought their owner to his door, to see what his hunters had treed. When he discovered us, a squad of mounted yanks, he kicked and cuffed his

Canines into silence. Then we asked him where we were at, and were very muched "*pleased*" to learn, we were about three miles out of our way, which reminded me, of the old saying, that short cuts on a strange country are generally a long way round. However he told us of a short cut by which we could reach our destination. We are dubious of short cuts, but it was now far into the night, so we concluded to give it a trial. A heavy frost was on the ground and the moon was well up over head. This time we came out all right, but were rather uncertain as to whether we would find any body up, as it was about eleven o'clock.

There was a dim light struggling through a curtain, which was over the single front window of the log house; quiet reigned about the lonesome place until we were discovered by the usual number of cur dogs that seem to be always in force at these country abodes. They greeted us with some yelps in do, ra, me, tones, which brought our host to the door. Baugher made himself known to his "relative" who then invited us to dismount and enter; we explained why were were so late. He said he had given us up. The ceremony had come off about nine o'clock. Most of the guests had gone home, also the fiddler; some young ladies still lingered, and the bride and groom regarded us bashfully. The ceremony of introductions was gone through in a hap hazzard manner. The bride is seventeen, while the groom is about two years older.

Some one suggested that we go and get the band and have a dance, which seemed to be favorably received by every one, so I volunteerd and took two of the boys. He lived only a mile off, and we covered the distance in quick time, found the place, a cabin in the woods, with not a sign of life about it, not even a dog to give us a welcome bark. Nothing daunted we thumped on the door. A voice from within wants to know, whose there. Telling him where we were from, he unbolted the door and invited us in. The place was in darkness, the wood fire in the fire place being banked up with ashes. He raked the ashes aside, and the fire blazed up, disclosing him in undress uniform just as he had got out of bed. The house had only the one room, and by the dim light of the fire, we discovered a couple of beds, one occupied by his wife. In the other was visible two black heads belonging to his grown up daughters; none of the quartet seemed to be at all embarrassed at our midnight intrusion. Mean time the old man was getting into his clothes while we explained matters. He did not at all object to go back with us, especially after it was suggested, his time would be liquidated with some of the present coin of the relm. He also said the girls might go too if they liked, and we were just about to beat a hasty retreat, thinking they might refuse to arise in our presence, but they declined, saying they were too tired. The old gent said he had a mule in the lean-to out side, and if we would saddle him, while he was getting ready, it would expedite matters; so we acted as groom for once, and brought the unwilling steed around. He dident seem to enter into the spirit of the occasion at all; we took care not to be to familliar with his mule ship, especially his business end; mules in general have a knack of introducing themselves to strangers by the back action of their heels. However our band was soon mounted with his instrament in a cottan bag tucked under his arm, and we rode back from whence we came, and ushered him in triumph within the waiting circle. The fun is about to commence, let joy be unrestrained.

Our band commenced to tune up. And we stood up in a double row, Baugher being master of ceremonies, with his fifty second cousin (the bride) for a partner. The groom stood with his back to the mantel, and dident seem to partake of the general joy, looked rather gloomy; in fact, I guess he wished we had stayed away. If he had the least bit of humor about him, he would soon have had the laugh on us. Allready, and the band began to play, and we started in to shake the light fantastic toe, as it were. But the tune and time, that greeted our ears, was as greek to the Egyptians, and we were in confusion in no time. There wasent a dragoon among us that knew what to do; the band paused to enquire whats the matter; we asked him to play something familliar, naming several dances, but we found he dident know a thing but the wheezy old dead and gone tune he was playing. He was as bad as the old Coon Skin in Arkansas, who could only play the first half of the Arkansas traveler. One of the boys said he could play a square dance, but after snapping two of the strings trying to get the thing up to the proper key, he gave it up in disgust. And so ended our anticipated frolic in a decided fizzle, and we chewed the cud of bitter disappointment, as there seemed to be nothing else in sight to chew in the way of edibles, or nothing to wet our whistles with either, we paid the band for his broken strings and time, and as there seemed to be nothing further to amuse us, we bid the host and the rest good by. We straddled our impatient animals and departed, about the sma' hour of one.

We enlivened the homeward gallop, by poking fun at Baugher; asked him about his uncles Aunts and Cousins, and other relatives, which he took in good part. We reached quarters tired and sleepy, after our more than twenty miles ride just as day began to lighten up the eastern sky.

24th I have been thinking of my poor old Will today. Will Sutcliffe, who was captured at the battle of Franklin; he was yanked from behind the breastworks, by the rebels; he stuck to his post a moment too long, and was taken prisoner. Our rallying force which drove the rebels out again, came a moment too late to save him. I suppose he is languishing in that death trap, Andersonville, where it is said, many a man who was unable to stand the torture and starvation inflicted upon them, had deliberately crossed the dead line, knowing it was instant death; knowing that his brutal guards would shoot him down at once; preferring a quick death, to lingering torture and final ending.

If all the stories told of this terrible place are only half true, it is small wonder that many of the prisoners loose their reason, and seek a quick death at the hands of their guards, thus ending their misery. With no shelter from the hot broiling sun at midday, or from the down pour of storms, with hardly enough to eat to keep body and soul together, I sincerely hope my friend Will, will escape with his life.

25th We had quite an exciting time today. Fire was discovered on the second floor, over our office. The family who occupy the east wing, got into a frantic state thinking they would be burned out of house and home.

Our office force turned ourselves into an impromtu fire brigade at once, calling for all the buckets about the premises, filling them from the cistern. I got an ax and pryed up the flooring and the fire was quickly drowned out with slight damage. The female portion of the family were very profuse in their thanks, which we took in with proper modesty, but the truth was we were as anxious as they, not to be turned out of our comfortable quarters.

Feb 3d My old chum and bunk mate turned up today, after an absence of about fourteen months, in several rebel prisons. He was captured during the second day's battle of Chickamauga 20th Sept

1863, when I came so near falling into the hands of the enemy, together with a couple hundred others, we being cut off from our lines. Fortunately for us, we defeated the force sent to take us in, turning the tables on them, by capturing many of them, whom we could only disarm and turn loose again, as we were several miles south of the enemys lines. Morse entertained us with a vivid description of his experience; had been taken from one prison to another, each worse than the last, and was half starved in all of them. He was nearly eaten up in all of them by the vermin that swarm in all the prison holes. Indeed his frame gave evidence of great shrinkage. He looked like the famous skeleton that was said, was drawn through a knot hole.

We promised to feed him up, and get his constitution into its old time condition, but he said he only came to get his furlough, which is granted to all returned prisoners in his condition.

He said his principal diet was stale corn bread and hope, the latter he had to supply himself; many a poor fellow had succumbed when his supply of hope had given out.

Morse said, he had about become ripe for a southern grave, and was getting ready to wrap the mantle of despair about his shakey frame, and give up the ghost, when one day he had the luck to be called, and join a batch of prisoners for exchange. He said he was as weak as a starved cat, the joyful news nearly upset him.

6th Lakey, Perviance, Baugher and myself are notified that we may be called as witnesses in a case to come up before a sitting Court Marshall at Decatur Ala, but are left in the dark as to the nature of the trial, and can not imagine what we know about it, what ever it is.

Mch 8th I have decided to apply for a furlough, and take a trip north; if I can get our Genl Elliotts endorsement, it will go through. Ordinarily the course of an application, is through the A A G's office, that is our office to Capt Jacobs[2], our A.A.G. But as none of us care to ask a favor of him, he being unpopular among his subordinates, I take my written application to Capt Sibley, who readily endorses it with his approval. Then I present it personally to the Genl. who takes charge of it with a promise to send it forward approved, so half the battle is won at the start. And as the fate of such a request generally depends upon the first two or three endorsements, it is pretty sure to come back granted, after ascending step by step through the various degrees to Department Hd Qrs. Why do I want a furlough? Why I want to get back to civilized life again if only for a limited time. The war is virtually over, here in the west at least, and will soon end in the east, with

[2]This captain was Jesse Elliott Jacobs of Pennsylvania. He became a captain in July of 1862, was breveted Major and Lt. Colonel in March, 1865, and on the same day Colonel, for faithful and meritorious service during the war. Each reader may decide for himself the degree to which captain Jacobs persecuted private Smith.

Sherman on the south of Richmond and Grant on the north it's only a matter of time when Lee and Johnson will capitulate; and then, peace once more.

20th I receive orders to go to Nashville and bring back some books and records belonging to our Hd-Qrs. Procuring transportation &c. I board an out going train. The R R is in horrible condition, the rails are bent into hills and hollows, and we bump along over them in momentary expectation of being dumped in the ditch.

21st Reach my destination, and climb out of the freight car, pulling myself together to be sure my bones are all intact and no joints dislocated, or shook loose. I present my credentials to the Post Q.M. and secure the desired articles.

23d Am back again once more, and feel as though I had gone through a campaign; I think it will take a week to get my anatomy into its normal condition, one of the cars, caught fire from a hot box on the forward part of the train, and was well under way before it was discovered. Stoping near a ditch with water in it, the crew soon had the fire out.

25th Mch Orders recd. to break up camp and move to East Tenn. and perhaps on through West Virginia; sufficient cars are provided to convey our division, bag and baggage, and we are soon en route for Chattanooga.

29th We have passed through C- via Stevenson Ala. & Loudon Tenn. and arrive at Knoxville, where we disembark. A curious freak of nature, or the elements, transpired, a puzzler for the gray heads of science; Robt Smith, Dink and myself, were standing near the head car of our train, the engine having left us, when of a sudden, one of the most terrific thunder storms came up, or down more properly speaking. We three sought shelter beneath the car, to await its passing. Brilliant flashes of lightning, and most deafening peals of thunder followed. While we sat with our knees under our chins gazing up the track, a terrific crack of thunder, occurred, accompanied by a flash that lit up the universe, it struck between the rails some distance up the track, and a ball of fire, or bolt of lightning or what ever it was, about the size of a bullet, came down the track, like a shot from a rifle, passing lengthwise under the car where we sat; in fact it passed between us, and we felt the heat on our faces, as it passed with a hiss like the sound of a bullet. It exploded just beyond us, making a sound like the firing of a musket. The air was filled with a sulphorous smell; our first impulse was to dodge and dive out into the deluge, but we were paralized as by an electric shock, to say we were startled, would poorly express our sensations; we were scared, and no mistake, and decided unanimously we had had the closest shave of the war, from being totally annihilated. I was forceably reminded of my experience upon the Cumberland Mountains in the clouds.

April 1st Following the line of R R. by easy marches we arrive at Bulls Gap, in the mountains near West Virginia. In the mail which was received this evening, my furlough came to me approved, Amen. Perviance also recd. one for twenty days, and we conclude to travel to civilization in company.

April 3d We bid good by to the mess, and take the cars for Chattanooga. On arriving we are greeted by the glorious news, that Richmond had fallen, with no particulars however. But this much was enough to send us on our way rejoicing, for was it not a presage of the end of the war, and another victory for Grant, and the army of the Potomac. The troops in the east have been battering away at the portals of the Capital City of the Confederacy for more than four long years.

6th Perviance and I, land in Louisville Ky. and here we part company, he going on to his home, and I continue on towards Chicago.

8th Reaching my destination as hungry as a hunter, I hunt up Andersons restaurant on Clark near Randolph St determined to get out side of a good square breakfast. Entering the open portals of the palace of porter house steaks &c, I ran up against a great and pleasurable surprise, in the form of an old and valued friend, none other then Chas R Sanders, (Cal)[3]. I was struck all of a heap as the saying is, having lost sight of him for many moons, and

---

[3] It is hard to know just what Smith means here. The official records of the Illinois Adjutant General report that Calvin Smith deserted October 19, 1864. Whether Private Smith is, with his tongue in his cheek, describing a meeting with his

did not know whether he was in the land of the living or not. The pleasure of our unexpected encounter, I dare say was mutual; I enjoyed my breakfast with great relish, while mutual explanations followed. His regiment was stationed here and making preparations to depart for the Western plains, to take care of the restless indians. After my breakfast we went over to the Central Hotel, I engaged a room, and then we took a stroll about town, and down to the lake front. At the noon hour we went back to my hotel and had dinner, after which he returned to his camp.

April 10th Confirmation and particulars of the capture of Richmond continue to arrive. Lee evacuated, and our troops took possession. This means that the cruel war is nearing its end, for Lees army out side of their citadel will soon be compelled to capitulate. General rejoicing is the order of the day; rejoicing is not unmixed with sadness, when one remembers the thousands of stout hearts and willing hands, that marched away from home and friends; that went away to fight for the liberties of the free'st country on earth; that sacrificed their lives for freedoms cause, whose bones now lie burried in the far off south, on the battle field and plain, with scarce a mound to mark the spot where they fell.

brother, or whether there was a real "Charles R. Sanders (Cal)," is now impossible to determine. If this is brother Calvin, perhaps after his defection, he did enlist in a different regiment, one destined to go west and fight Indians.

Chapter X

*Wherein Smith is on furlough in Chicago; it is here
he learns the shocking news of Lincoln's assassina-
tion. After a visit to Kankakee, Smith goes boating
on Lake Michigan and barely reaches shore safely
when a storm comes up. On May 1 he joins the
long, silent line that passes before Lincoln's body
lying in state at City Hall. When his furlough ends,
he reports to division headquarters near Nashville;
after several serious disagreements with Assistant
Adjutant General Jacobs, he is relieved from headquarters duty and ordered to return to Company C
of the 51st Illinois Infantry. The next day, however,
in spite of Captain Jacobs, he is assigned to department headquarters in Nashville. In Nashville he
enjoys an easy, pleasant life, and is often able to go
to the theatre; once he falls down a roof while fighting a fire, but he lands without injury; later he
succumbs to the craze of autograph collecting.
Granted another furlough, Smith reaches Chicago
on August 3 but decides to go East. After seeing
the sights in New York, he goes on to Providence,
Rhode Island. Here he finds life a steady round of
parties and excursions, and overstays his leave. After
visiting Bunker Hill he heads back to Nashville
and more easy occupation duty, interrupted by*

*the execution of the guerilla Champ Ferguson.
On November 3, learning that his regiment is being
mustered out, Smith applies for a discharge, is
ordered to Springfield, Illinois, and is mustered out
of the army on November 7, 1865; his journal
ends in Chicago on the next day.*

April 15th The city is in a ferment of excitement.
Groops of citizens are congregated upon every street
corner discussing the all absorbing topic of news.
The telegraph reports that our President Lincoln
has been shot, assassinated while sitting in a box at
Fords Theatre in Washington. Expressions of anger,
and horror, mingled with sorrow are heard upon all
sides. Indignation in deepest terms is heard from
every one. To think that just as the angel of peace
was about to spread its white wings over our country, the Angel of death steps in and cuts short the
life of our nations best friend. Just as the light of
day is about to dawn upon, the close of the long
struggle, death should claim our Noble President
for its victim, just as he was prepared to enjoy the
fruits of a noble and unselfish career. The saving of
a nation, and striking off the chains that bound the
lives of millions of slaves, making them free: "Oh!
justice where art thou, that you have been blinded,
and allowed this thing to be, Justice!, go and hide
your face for very shame. Why did you let this
monster to be begot, why allow him to be fostered

among men, that it was not strangled at its birth, did you not know that it would fasten its villainous clutch upon the throat of an innocent victim, and destroy a man as far above him, as a white winged angel of Heaven, is above a black winged demon of the Nether regions?["]

But right here in our midst is three of the villains deciples. They walk the streets, shouting for joy that the innocent is slain. They cry 'tis good enough for him. The words falling upon the ears of excited citizens, is like unto burning tow applied to a barrel of gunpowder. They shoot[1] the villains so quickly, that the cry dies in their throats mingled with the death rattle. All three drop in their tracks, shot by men who love justice; the bodies lay there for some time, as a warning to those who may entertain like centiments. No one attempts to molest the slayers; the law takes no heed; the swift Justice is approved by all good citizens.

17th I take a run down to Kankakee, to see my old friends and neighbors, stay until the 22d and wished to remain longer, for all the young people, old friends, have entertained me royally. Upon reaching Chicago, Sanders met me and we take pot luck together, and stroll about town the rest of the day.

April 25th In a fit of lonesomeness a sort of

---

[1]None of the surviving Chicago newspapers mention these murders. This sounds like the kind of rumors that could have been current in Chicago on April 15th. Smith does not say that he either saw the shooting or the bodies.

dontknow what to doativeness comes over me;
mechanically I saunter down to the lake front, hire
a boat, and rowing out a mile or more from shore,
and rest upon my oars. The warm sun spreads its
rays over the bosom of the lake. Surrounded by the
calm waters no breath of air ripples its surface only
an easy long swell, like an incoming tide on the
ocean. Far away from the noise and turmoil of the
city, it is a place to rest and dream day dreams.
Looking northward over the vast expanse of this
inland sea, it is dotted here and there with black
hulls and white sails, of many ships; farther, as far
as the eye can reach, where the blue sky and blue
waters meet, the little black lines seemingly emerg-
ing from the water, with long black streamers of
smoke issuing from them, indicate steamers, while
issuing from the mouth of the river, are the swift
gray hounds of the lake, the pilot tug boats, darting
swiftly after their prey, the vessels they tow into
port. Taking no heed to the passage of time, I am
suddenly brought to realize that the wind is rising,
by the sound of the little choppy ripples that knock
against the sides of my boat. Looking towards the
east I discover a low bank of clouds capped with
black heads, which means, a squall is coming up if
no worse, and being aware its no joke to be caught
out on the lake in a storm, in a small row boat, I
conclude to make tracks for terra-firma. As my boat
raced over the water under a long steady pull, I
could see the long rolling swells coming towards me

showing their teeth, of white foam, as though the mighty waters were taking deep breath, as if preparing itself for the mighty struggle with the storm king. How like unto the human race, is the warring of the elements; how like an army of soldiers, calmly marching forward, with no disturbing element in sight, carelessly they move along, when suddenly, perhaps unexpectedly, the enemy turns up. Then every one is on the alert; the preliminary commotion is started, the excitement of anticipation prevails. The first volley is fired, and the human strife begins; one body of men will charge, as though they would fly at the throats of the enemy, with a chorus of yells that awaken the echoes. The keel of my boat grates upon the shore, and none too soon; the big drops of rain commence to fall, and the wind is lashing the waves into foaming crests.

May 1st The remains of our late President arrived today and was escorted by a vast number of citizens from the funeral train to the corridor of the City Hall, where lying in state, it was viewed by thousands, who slowly file by the bier. Getting into the line, I look upon the still form and calm features of our Lincoln, lying in his narrow bed. There passed through my mind, thoughts of the greatness which so recently animated that silent form; the grand achievements so nearly completed, the lasting results of which will embalm his memory in the hearts of his fellow men.

As I gaze upon the homely features, so still and

motionless, homely in life, beautiful in death, I think of the honest old Abe whom the soldiers loved so well. Soon he will be laid away in his silent tomb, there to await his final reward at the hands of his Master, "May his soul rest in peace."

May 5th My furlough is about to expire, and I must turn my face towards the sunny south, once more. Thanks to the powers that be, it is not likely to be for long. Friend Sanders accompanies me to the depot, and I depart on the evening train.

7th Reach Nashville without incident, and learn our division has returned from East Tenn. and gone into camp near town; ascertaining their whereabouts, I hasten to report for duty, reaching Head Quarters in the midst of a severe rain storm. The boys welcome me back among them; by the time they all got through shaking my hand, I thought I should have to send my arm to the hospital for general repairs. They also gave me a friendly warning to be very circumspect in the presence of our noble A A G. Capt Jacobs, whom it seems has developed into tyrannical ways, with those immediately under his supervision.

May 16th I am in correspondence with J Middleton Arnold formerly of this office, who was promoted to Capt Porters office, at Hd. Qrs. Mil. Div. of the Tenn., Genl Geo H Thomas Commanding, with a view to succeed him there, as he has been commissioned as Major, and appointed A A G of the State of Tenn, Parson Brownlow Governer;

Our J. E. J. is becoming more aggressive day by day.

25th The climax was reached today, when with no just provocation from my point of view, The Great Captain opened up the batteries of his wrath upon me, before the whole office. Without thinking of the consequences, I sent it back to him in equal force, greatly to the amazement of the rest of the boys, and did not show the best of good sense on my part, considering our difference in rank, but only put the Captain in a white heat, and I was immediately placed under arrest.[2] And one of the boys was directed to make an official order which he signed, ordering me to report at once to my company, in the old 51st. I might have made an appeal personally to Genl Elliott, being well satisfied he would reverse his Capt. judgement, but as my application to Department Hd Qurs was pending, I concluded not to force the matter into more importance. I bid the boys good by and departed, for my regiment. Explaining matters to Capt Tilton, he told me to take it easy pending events.

26th My official documents arrived from Nashville today. I am ordered to report forthwith for duty; taking in Div. Hd Qrs on my way, the boys congratulate me on my promotion, also said that after I had departed the day before, a paper had

[2]There is no mention in the Illinois Adjutant General's records concerning his arrest and return to the 51st. But Civil War records leave much to be desired, and there is no good reason to doubt Smith's story.

reached there for indorsement, as to my charactor, ability &c. The Captains province was to endorse, and return it, which he did with a vengeance, as he was still in his wrath towards me. The boys said the paper was returned with an endorsement covering all the available space, and gave me a charactor, stubbornness, insubordination &c too numerous to mention. They thought my case was surely settled, but my Major out ranked the Captain; besides he knew me thoroughly, in fact we were old chums, so the endorsement of our doughty Capt. was ignored, and the order sent at once. Of course it went through Div Hd Qrs, and through Jacobs hands; imagine his feelings, at the impotancy of his wrath. I went to Nashville and reported at once. After being introduced to Capt L L Porter, in charge, the Major initiated me into his late position, placing me in charge of the furlough records.

The Major had a laugh over Capt Jacobs unworthy endeavor and we smiled as we recalled the episode of the calf one certain midnight not so many moons past. Then we walked down to the Hotel-de-Cumberland, introduced me to his old mess. This is a convenient building erected by order of Genl Thomas for the accomodation of all Hd Qur. clerks. My duties are of a much more responsible character than at Div Hd Qrs, but the pay is three times as much; the office hours are from 9 to 12, and 1:30 to 4 P.M. The rest of the time is our own to use or abuse as we see fit.

June 1st After office hours, I straddle a horse, and take a run out to my old Div. Hd. Qrs. and call upon the boys, who insist upon my taking pot luck with them; spent a pleasant evening, and gave them a general invite to take supper with me at the Hotel-de-Cumberland.

June 9th A Fire started in our block at the upper end, about one o'clock P.M. today, in Taylors Depot of supplies. We all turned out to see it. Finding it under such head way, that our office was in serious danger, several of us got upon the roof of the next building, which was a three story dwelling, with a sharp steep roof; there was another roof about a story lower in the back yard with only one long slant towards the inner yard. Buckets of water were drawn up by ropes, and we wet down the smoking shingles, until the roof was as slippery as glass; while changing position on the comb of my high perch, I made a misstep, and shot down the roof at a 2.40 gait. With nothing to stay my progress I shot over the eves down on to the lower roof, with presence of mind enough to light on my toes, and thus break the shock a little; a big fellow made a grab for me, but miscalculated the force of my fall; he was tripped up, and we both sat down with more force than elegance. This roof being as slippery as the other, we stopped not upon the order of our going, but went at once; down we slid, over the eves we shot, and landed upon the hard ground; again I break the jar by striking upon my toes first, and so sustained only a good shaking up, while my would be preserver being a two hundred pounder, landed much heavier, and flat footed. Dont think he was much hurt, as he was able to rip out a few short ejaculations, more forcible than choice. I took in the rest of the show from the spectators stand point, while I reflected upon the lucky fact, that my slip occurred on the inner slant of the upper roof instead of the outer, in which case I would have fallen three stories, and landed on a stone pavement, and no doubt my career as a fireman and soldier would have come to an abrupt end. My epitaph might have read something like this: he took a toboggan slide, into eternity. The fire was quenched after it had consumed Taylors place and five dwellings; a few more and we would have been turned out of our Hd Qrs.

June 11th Another fire occurred today a greater one than that of the 9th. The fire department is in better shape now; I with several of the boys, stood in the usual crowd of spectators. The pipe man incidently turned his nozzle our way, and we got a ducking, in fact a good soaking, so we had to go to our abode and change clothing throughout.

20th An alarm of fire sounded after dark, several of us started for the scene of action, and found an officer lying insensible in the gutter, where he had fallen from his horse. A hook and ladder co had collided with him. We picked him up and took him into the nearest house, while one of the boys ran to

HdQrs for the surgeon, who came at once, and soon brought the victim back to his senses, but he had to be sent to the hospital.

July 4th This is the 89th anniversary of the Declaration of Independence. At day light the forts around the outskirts of the city awoke the echos, by firing a national salute. It reminded me forcibly of the 15th of last December, the racket and roar of the big guns, only now they are all blanks that are fired.

27th The daily routine of my office, while it is not of an exacting nature, except as to promptness in its hours. At 4 P.M. we quit for the day, and I spend a good deal of my spare time in reading. I am deeply interested in a book now, entitled The Prince of the House of David.[3] A young Jewess goes to Jerusalem on a visit to some relatives; she writes letters to her father, relating passing events, it being at the time of the advent of Christ. The letters take the form of a narative, and gives one an interesting history of passing events in and around Jerusalem.

A craze has broken out among the boys in the several offices of the Department, that is to secure the autographs of all the great men, and big guns generally that occupy commanding stations around us. I secure a lot, headed by the most illustrous among them, Genl Geo. H Thomas Comdg. Dep. of

[3] J. H. Ingraham, *The Prince of the House of David; or, Three Years in the Holy City* (New York: Pudney and Russell, 1857).

the Tenn., Parson Brownlow Gov. of Tenn, and state Treasurer Stanford and many others too numerous to mention. I conclude to apply for a leave of absence for thirty days, so I lay the matter before our worthy Capt. Porter, charge-de-affairs of our office; he being of a most kindly-nature undertakes to put it through for me.

31st The Capt. handed me my furlough, duly signed by the commander in chief. Making an entry of it in my big folio, the last until my return, I turn my desk and duties over to Armstrong, pack my grip and after bidding the boys good by, start on my way to Chicago once more.

Aug 3d Making a quick trip, without a stop or lay over, I reached Chicago this morning and put up at the Central House.

7th I have paid a round of visits to all my friends, and conclude to make a flying visit to Providence R.I., securing a birth in a sleeping car through to NY.

9th Arrive at the great metropolis this morning, and spend the day sight-seeing. Visit Central Park, Barnums Museum and the Broadway museum of anatamy. At 5 P.M. I get aboard a sound steamer of the Neptune Line. After supper, with my cigar, I promenade the deck, enjoying the salt sea breeze, and watch the lights of the fast receeding City, as we steam along Long Island Sound. Growing tired of this I seek my birth and turn in, and soon fall into the arms of Morpheous.

10th The Steamer made her wharf about six A.M. Landing I hunted up a restaurant and ordered breakfast principally oysters this being a favorite dish of mine. Then boarding a street car, I soon landed in Cranston, and make my appearance before the astonished gaze of Sister Mary, who exclaims in the first breath, Benshe-li-am a name associated with me while in short frocks, curly hair and Juvenility.

20th The past ten days, have been red letter days of enjoyment. All whom I have come in contact seem to have tried to make my stay among them, as pleasant as possible. Social gatherings at the house music and mirth, the rides through the moonlight delivering our load of Jolly couples to their several homes in the City, a day on the beach, with an old fashioned clambake, boating and bathing. Each gathering marked by its own amusements, Crowding in a months pleasures into ten days; variety is the spice of life, they say. There has been all the variety one could desire. The weather has been all that we could wish for.

23d Joe, his better half, and myself, made a trip to Boston, visiting the Museum. The large building contains as great a variety of curiosities as it has been my good fortune to see. We spent several hours inspecting its several departments. Its great variety of curios is both instructive and amusing. Its cases are filled with hundreds of skeletons, of birds and beasts and also of the human family, from many climes; specimins of minerals from every where on the globe. The vegitable and floral exhibit, is not one of the least. A specimen of the Mermaid with a head about the size and shape of a sun dried monkey of the ugliest type, with the body swallowed by the latter part of a fish; Joe said it was manufactured to order, no doubt of that, Nature would blush to produce any thing so ugly. At noon tide, we all agreed we were hungry. Turning our backs upon the representations of a pre-historic age, we hunted up a place very much of the present age, ordered dinner for three. After dinner, we separated to meet again at the depot at train time. I took a street car for Charleston, getting off at the street leading up to Bunker Hill monument. Reaching the entrance, I was met by the custodion, who politely requested me to register which I did, in a huge volume, think-ing my name would be swallowed up instantly among the ten thousand preceding me. Twenty cents please, said my worthy janitor, and I went down into my pocket, and tendered the shekels.

Within the central space at the base of the granite pile, is a life sized statue of General Warren, in white marble, representing one of the heroes that defended the hill from the repeated attacks of the red coats, in that time that tried men's souls. Climb-ing the granite circular stairway to the top, count-ing two hundred and ninety seven steps; this Cham-ber will hold a number of people. The view from each of the four openings is truly magnificent and one is well repaid after his hard climb. Leisurely enjoying the great panorama which covers a mighty distance, in all directions, full of life and teeming humanity; to describe its beauties is far beyond my power, while I fully appreciated the scene. But time and tide waits for no man, so I descend and make my way to the B & M depot, and find Joe and his wife waiting for me. Boarding the train, in one and a half hours we are crossing the bridge spanning the old Merrimac River at Haverhill, the old river where in I have so often sported and where my early career came very near being cut short one time by breaking through the ice, near the mouth of Little River. On a certain Saturday afternoon, a crowd of us boys was on the ice, just below Little River bridge. There was a rotten place in the ice which none of the boys dare cross. I with no judgment, and less wisdom, made a dash, and down I went, through the ice. As the river was ten or more feet deep, at that place, I went in up to my neck, over coat and boots on; being an expert swimmer for a boy it did not scare me a bit, but the boys danced around there, doing nothing, to help me, so I tried to get back on the ice, which would break through, and let me in again; this continued for quite a distance, until I hit some ice that the bridge shaded, and was thick enough to hold my weight. Then the boys helped me out. They took me under the arch of the bridge on to an old flat boat and with the thermometer ranging near zero, they stripped me to the skin, and wrung all the water out of every piece, and helped me on with them; then they hustled me on a run up and down until my blood was dancing. No bad effects followed. I did not even catch cold, but the next morning I did catch the whip on my bare legs.

31st Cousin Lucy and all her friends, have clubbed together to make our visit a pleasurable one. Pic-nic to Kinoza Lake, and Black Rock, excursions down the river to Plum Island below Newberry port Bay, a bathing party on the sandy shores of the old Atlantic; the Parties, composed of Lucy, Joe and his wife, sister Julia together with lots of the young people; we have all had a jolly time.

Sept 1st Back again in Providence and decide to stay another week.

7th I have overstayed my furlough, but the time has passed so swiftly, that it is hard to realize it. However I pull myself up short and decide to get back to my duties, as fast as steam will carry me. Bidding the good people farewell, at 5 P.M. I board a steamer for NY. While we were rounding Point Judith there was a fierce storm, and the waves rolled so high the Steamer pitched every which way. I had to brace myself in my birth or be pitched out on the floor.

9th Take the train for Cincinnati, passing through Albany, Rochester, Cleveland and Columbus, O.

11th At 12 M. take Steamer for Louisville, arriving on the 12th, at 6 A.M. Transfer to the L & N RR. Reach Nashville without incident and am once more within the walls of the Hotel-de-Cumberland, in good order.

Sept 13th Report my self to Capt Porter, who shook hands, and thats all he said about my being over due. I relieve Armstrong, and resume my old desk.

27th By a mutual friend, I am introduced to Capt Swisher, whose sister (Mrs Wright) is starring upon the boards of Duffield's Theatre. He becomes quite friendly, and gave me a general invitation to let him know when I want to visit the theatre, and passes for myself and any one of my friends will be forth coming.

Oct 11th Have attended the play frequently, in fact, have the run of the house, and my friend and chum, Congdon likewise. Waldron and I while taking a stroll this evening, met a friend, who invited us to go with him and witness a prize fight between two Buffalo experts. Neither of us having seen one fought by rules, conclude to go. The crowd we found congregated, was a pretty mixed one, some of them, had, "tough" written all over their features, and were easy to distinguish from the more respectable element. When time was called, the principals faced each other, striped to the waist. They were both fine specimens of muscular development. They fought a good many rounds, until one was knocked out, and failed to come up to the scratch when time was called; both their faces was a sight; resembled raw beefsteaks, well hammered; not an inviting sight by any means. But the general crowd seemed to appreciate the brutal sight, for they yelled themselves hoarse every time, a good blow was landed. For my part, this one experience, satisfied me.

20th Through the influence of Col Ramsey a party of us receive tickets of admission to the Yard of the penitentiary, to witness the execution by hanging, of the notorious guerilla and murderer Champ Ferguson. He has been convicted of all the worst crimes in the calendar, besides a score of cold blooded murders. At the appointed time, we go over to the prison, presenting our tickets, are assigned a position, just behind a single line of infantry, formed in a half hollow square around the scaffold. At the stroke of noon, the door of the jail was opened, the prisoner came out with a deputy on either side, a priest following with an open bible in hand. They moved forward with slow steps, the prisoner having his arms tied behind at the elbows. He is dressed in a new suit of black. Amid the perfect silence of the spectators, he mounted the steps, to the platform, seemingly with as much unconcern, as any one present, except his face was very white. He was placed upon the trap, the sheriff asked him if he had any thing to say; he answered so low we could not hear it. The rope was placed around his neck with the knot under his left ear. A black cap was then drawn over his head and face down to his chin, his feet tied together. The priest said a short prayer, Col Shafer read the sentence, and stepped aside. The sheriff took up a sharp hatchet, and delivered one blow on the rope that held the trap, which dropped; it, and the prisoner dropped about six feet, with a sickening thug, with his feet within a foot of the ground, the knees were slightly drawn up once and then fell. The Physician with his fingers on the pulse, in seven minutes, pronounced him dead. The body was cut down, the prison gates swing open, a wagon backed up, the remains was placed in a pine coffin, and the wagon drove away. Thus we saw the last of one of the worst desperadoes that Tenn. has produced.

23d The good people of this vicinity are greatly worked up, over a newspaper item, recently published. It came out in startling head lines, giving an account of the discovery of a hitherto unknown cave, situated under a portion of the city. It goes on to state that said cave is the rendezvoux of a band of robbers, which have been terrorizing belated people and stray soldiers, for the past several months. It is said the entrance or, open se-same of this robbers roost, is within the ghostly walls of one of the many old tombs in the cemetery. A wild and wooly romance eminating from the active brain of some penny a liner, no doubt, who is connected with the enter prising sheet. It is true however that a great many highway robbers are in active business in and around the City. They frequently maltreat their victims; now and then they encounter a belated soldier, and come out second best.

Nov 3d I learn through official sources that my regiment, that was sent with the brigade to Texas some time ago, have gone to Springfield, Ill, and been mustered out of the service, so I make application to be discharged. Transportation papers are promptly furnished; I also receive several letters of recommendation, as to habits, charactor and ability, and the kindly feeling of the donors; one from Maj. Genl. Geo. H. Thomas, Brig. Genl. Wm. B. Whipple, his Chief of Staff; also one from Capt. L. L. Porter, our office Chief. It being a spontaneous action on their part, I duly appreciate it. This being the eve of my departure, the boys get up an informal supper at the Hotel-de-Cumberland. Gathered about the festive board, we have nothing but excellent good feeling for each other; many are the good wishes expressed for our mutual prosperity, when we lay aside the blue, and assume the garb of the citizen. I am the youngest member of our mess, though none of the rest are much older, so we feel like a band of brothers. With a hand shake all round, not forgetting the ebony hued cook and his portly better half, or the small fry, who have kept our boots in proper shine, my grip being already packed, I hasten to the depot, and board the L & N train, and we are soon speeding Northward.

5th Reaching Springfield, the Capitol of the prairie state, register at the American House. After breakfast, I hired a buggy and drove out, to the sight of Lincolns tomb, at Oak Ridge. The body lies within a metalic case; within the tomb, a strong door of iron bars, guards the entrance, which is securely locked. The inner door is open, so one can see the interior and the casket. A soldier paces to and fro, guarding the place. He told me it is guarded day and night to prevent relic hunters from carrying off the whole thing piece meal. The tomb is built with large massive stones, which serve as a foundation for the large shaft that is being erected immediately over it; the sight is a beautiful one for the purpose.

7th Today I am a soldier no more.[4] I have crossed my last ditch, and entered the ranks of civil life. The Adjutant of the State presented me with my discharge papers, together with the sum that Uncle Sam owed me, and I turn my back upon the past. Four years and a month have I worn the blue, from seventeen to twenty one.

8th Again I am in Chicago, and for the last time I will scribble a line or two in my faithful journal, and then bid you farewell. You have been my constant companion for the past four years. I have guarded you as the apple of my eye, not knowing whether you would some day be finished completely or if per chance your career might be brought to a sudden end through the mishaps of war. My one

---

[4] According to the Illinois Adjutant General's records, Smith was mustered out of the army, being on detached service, September 25, 1865. The 51st Illinois had been sent to Texas in July, 1865 and was mustered out at Camp Irwin in that state September 25; the regiment arrived in Camp Butler at Springfield, Illinois on October 15 for final payment and discharge.

constant companion through out the struggle, in the peaceful camp, or on the silent picket line, tramping on foot or in the saddle, through sunshine and storm, you have stayed with me, when rations were short and when the Commissary was full to over flowing. On the field of battle when the deadly bullets flew too thick for comfort, or the screeching shell burst and scattered their ragged fragments around us, you were there too. And those times when you barely escaped with me, from falling into the hands of the enemy, in which case if I had survived the rebel prisons, you would no doubt have come to grief, as the rebs would have robbed me of your presence. Holding between your covers, a true history of passing events, if in future years I turn to your pages, seeking to refresh my memory, I will know your record is reliable.

B T SMITH

Index

INDEX

The Lakeside Classics